Valentine's Mandalas

Published by Hearth Write Press

307 E 4th Street

Bird City, KS 67731

Cover and interior design by DM Burns

All images sourced from Creative Fabrica.

Test Page

Use the icons below to test your tools before you begin coloring. You can try with markers, watercolors, glitter pens, whatever inspires you. Remember to check for bleed through on the back of the page. Happy coloring!

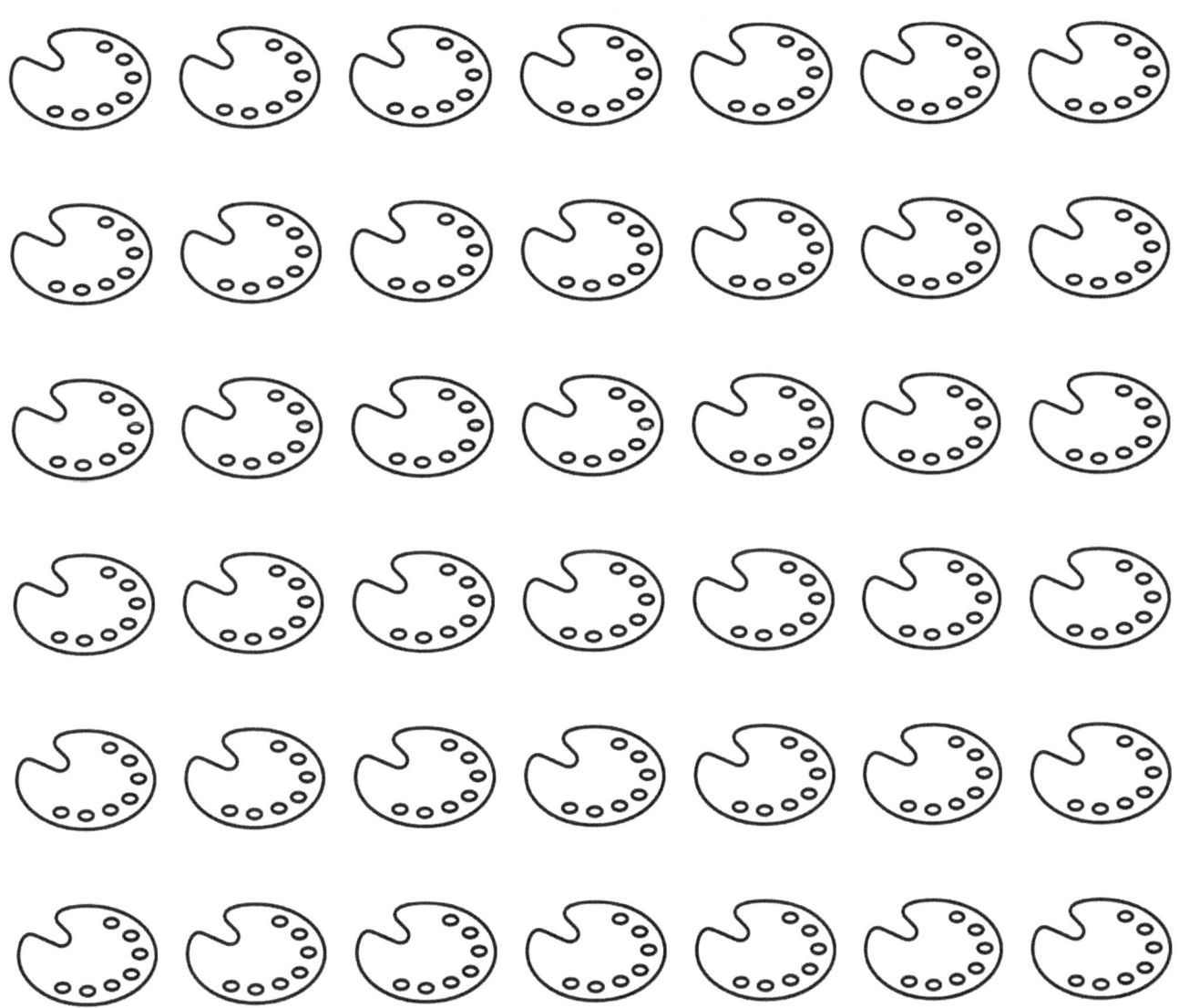

Test Page

Use the icons below to test your tools before you begin coloring. You can try with markers, watercolors, glitter pens, whatever inspires you. Remember to check for bleed through on the back of the page. Happy coloring!

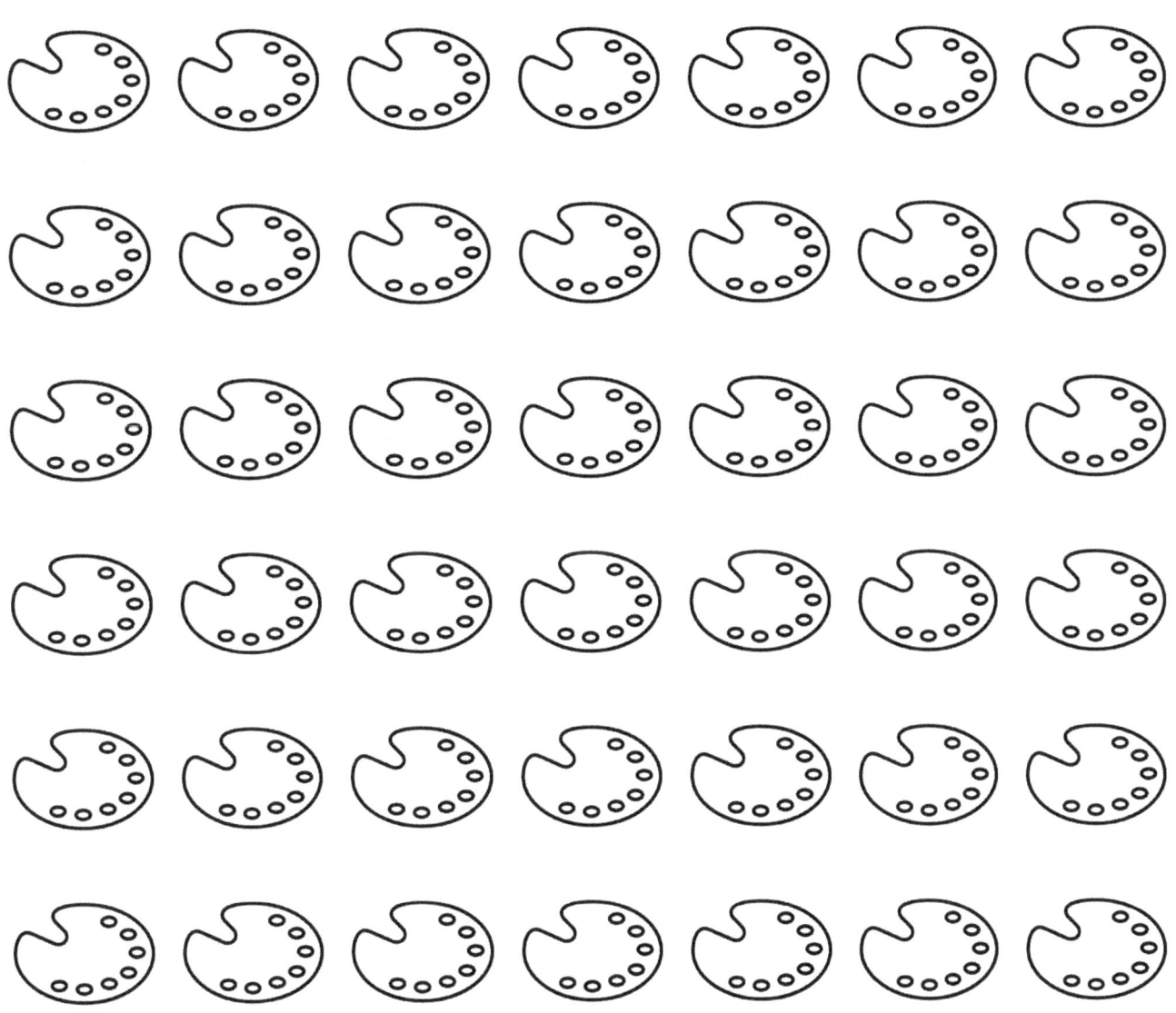

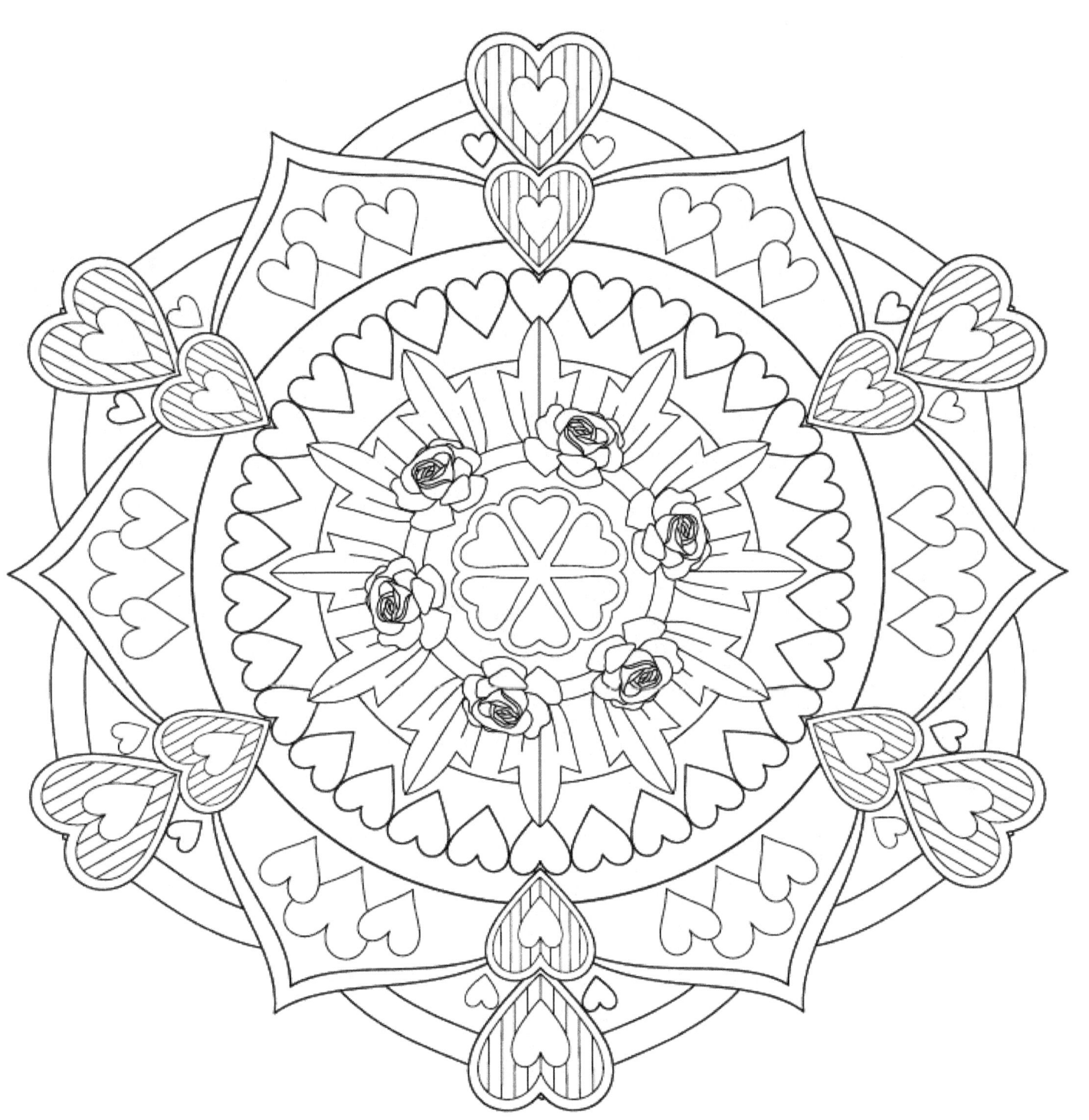

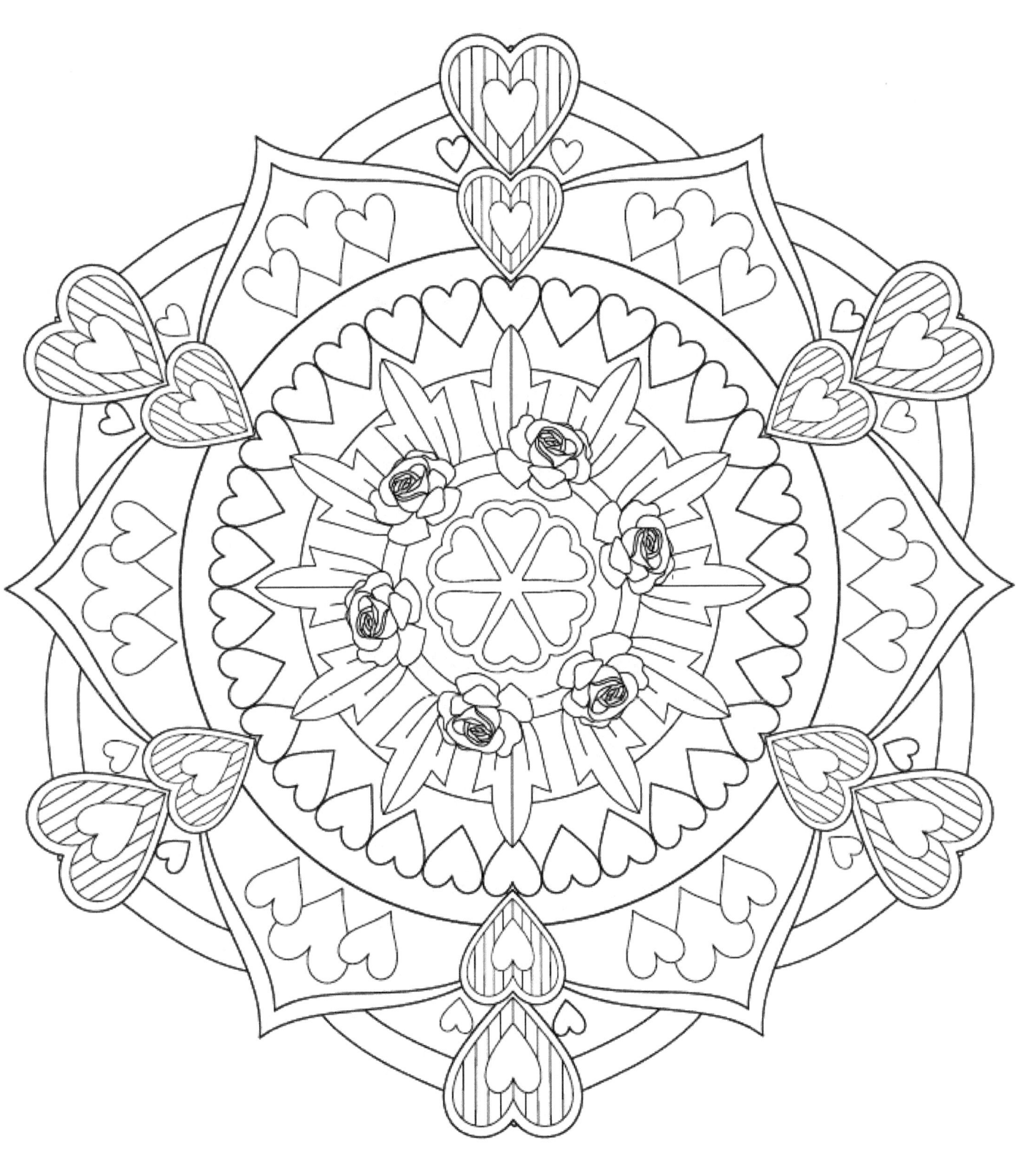

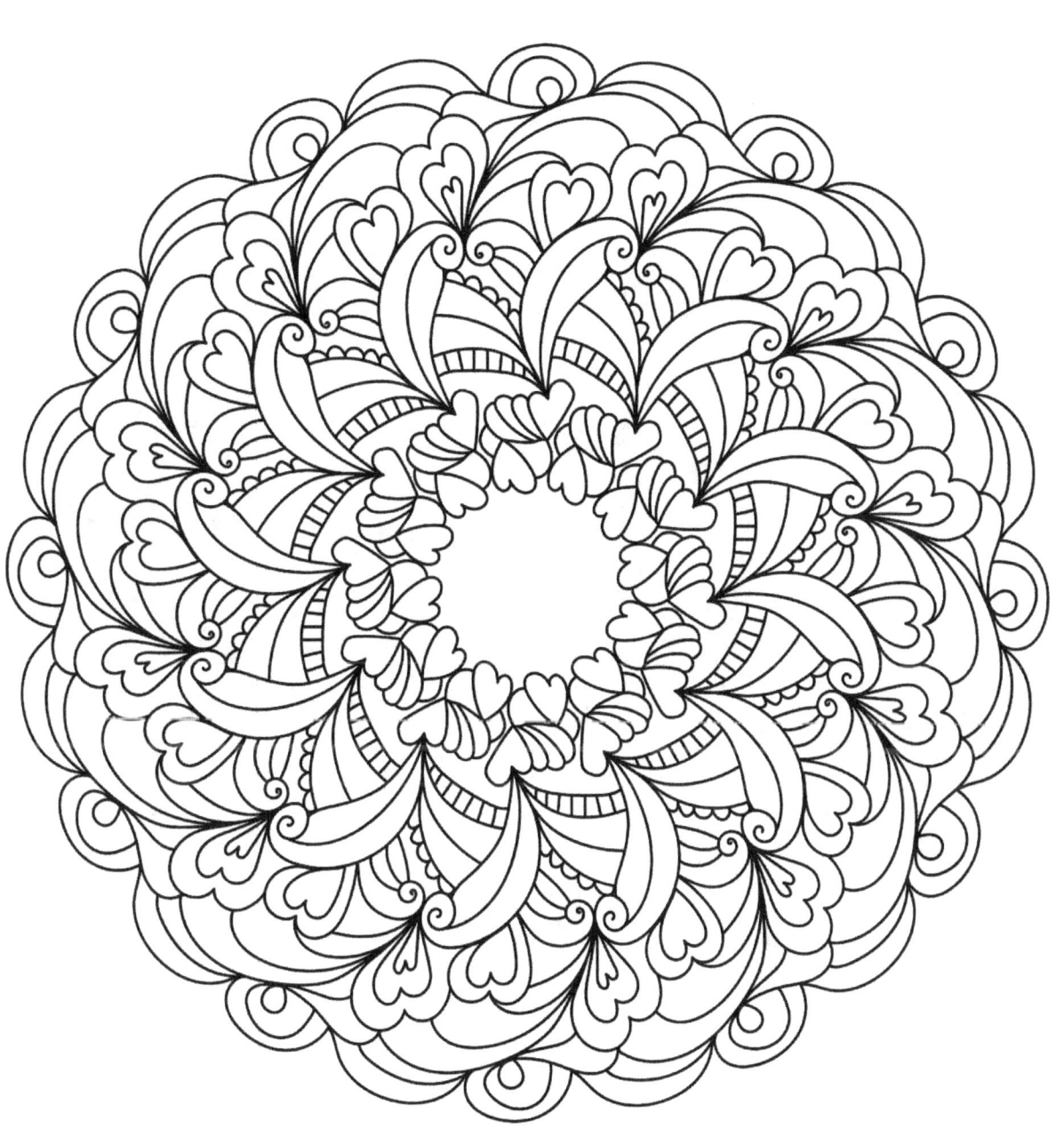

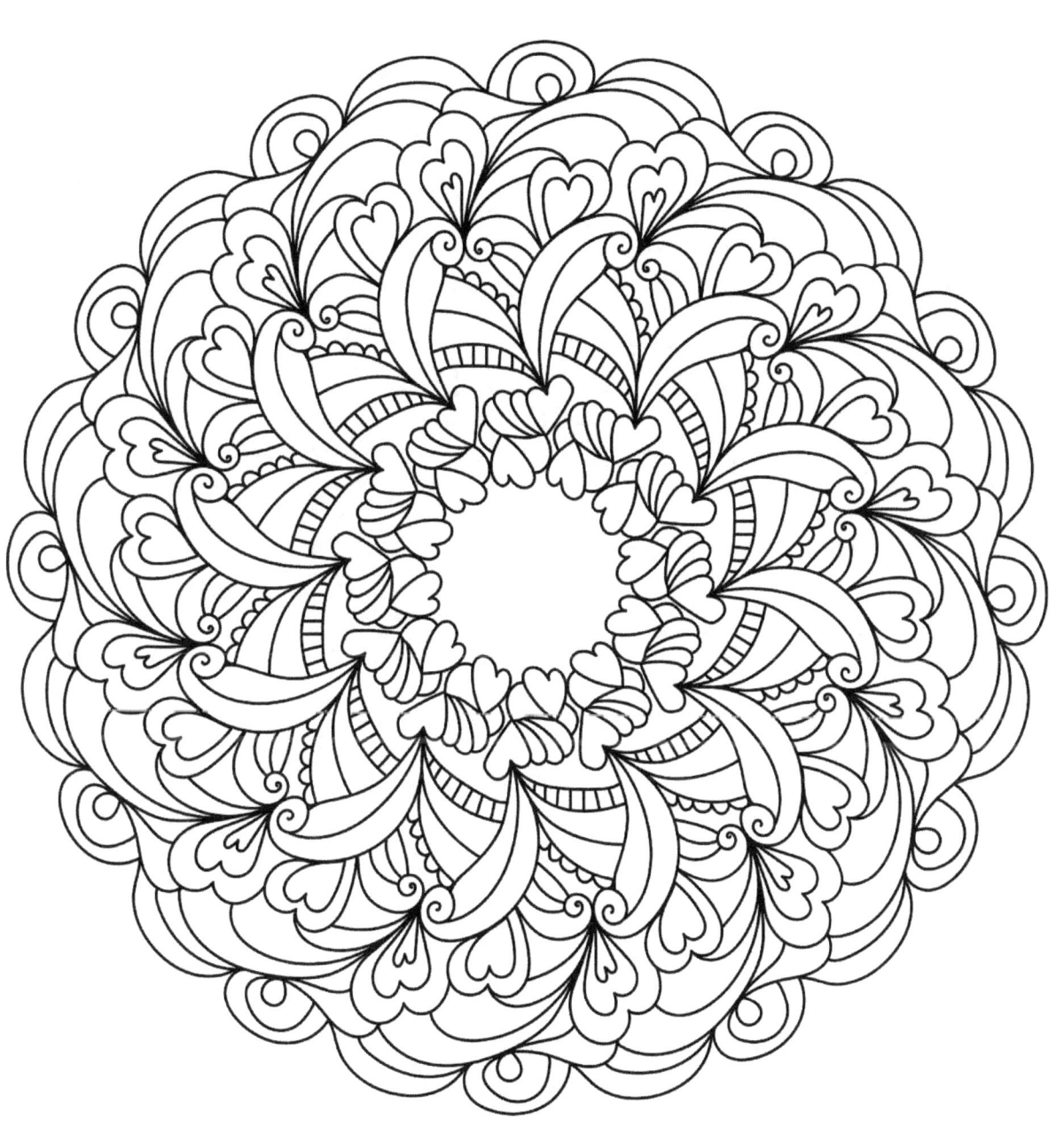

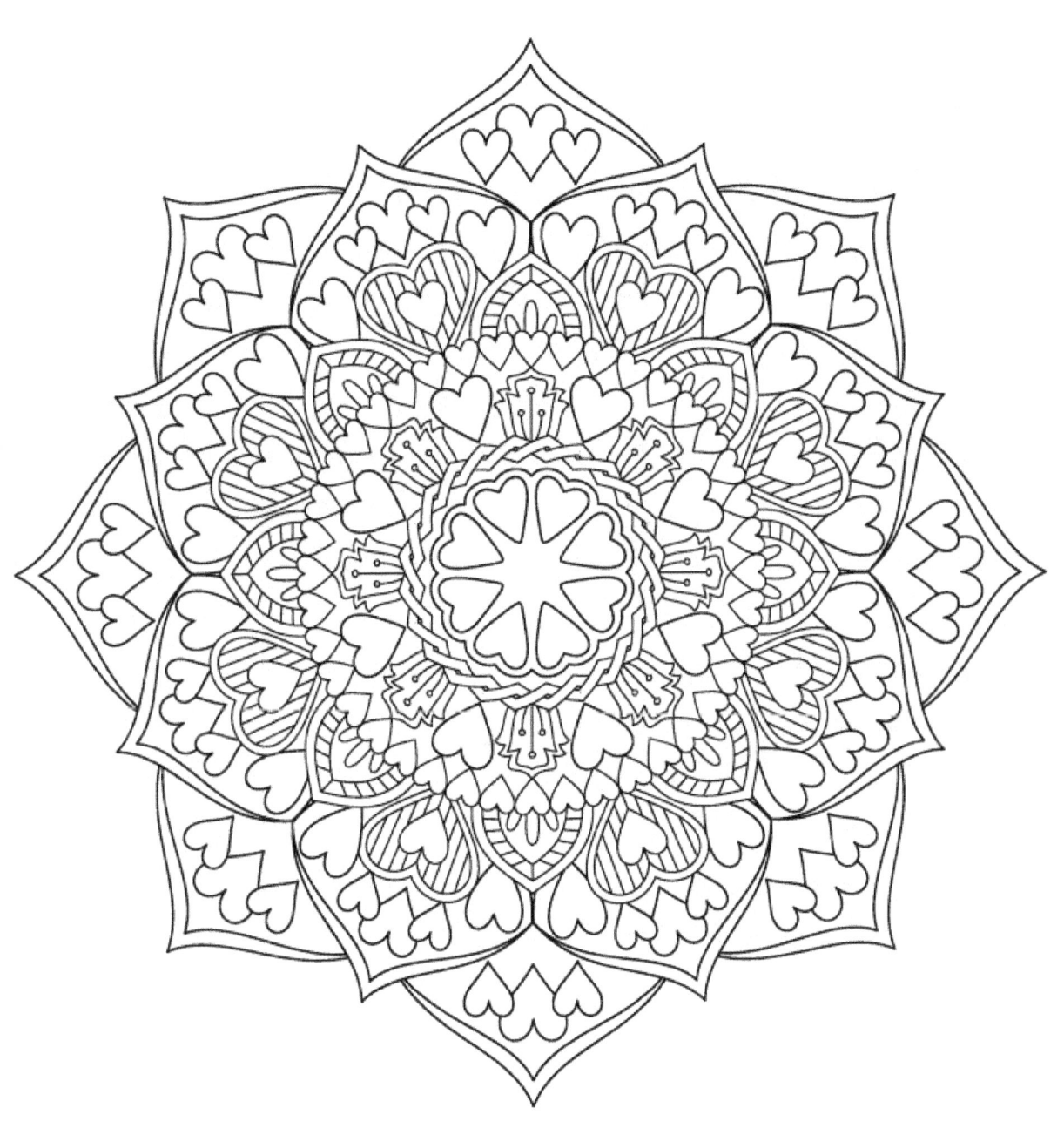

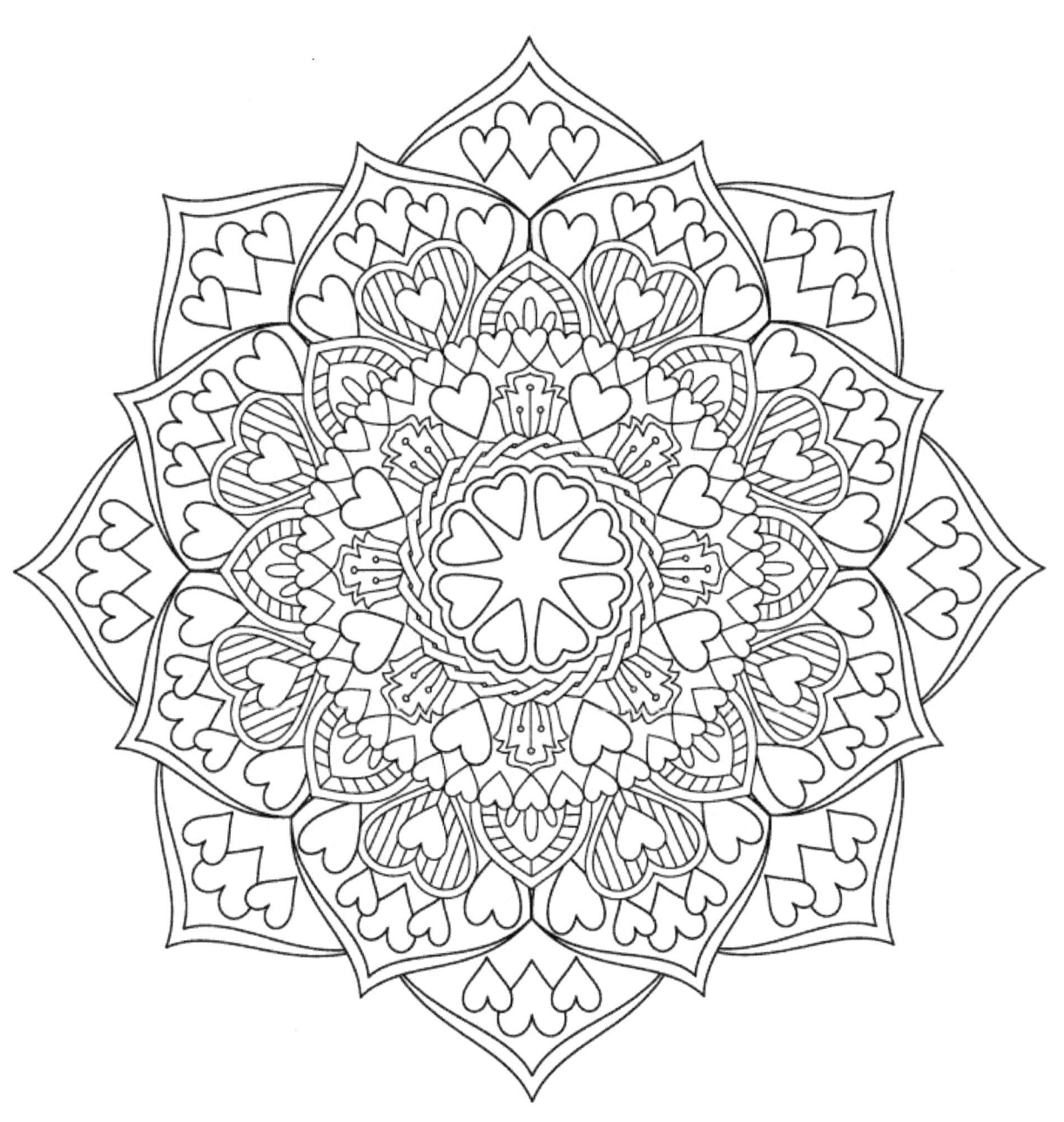

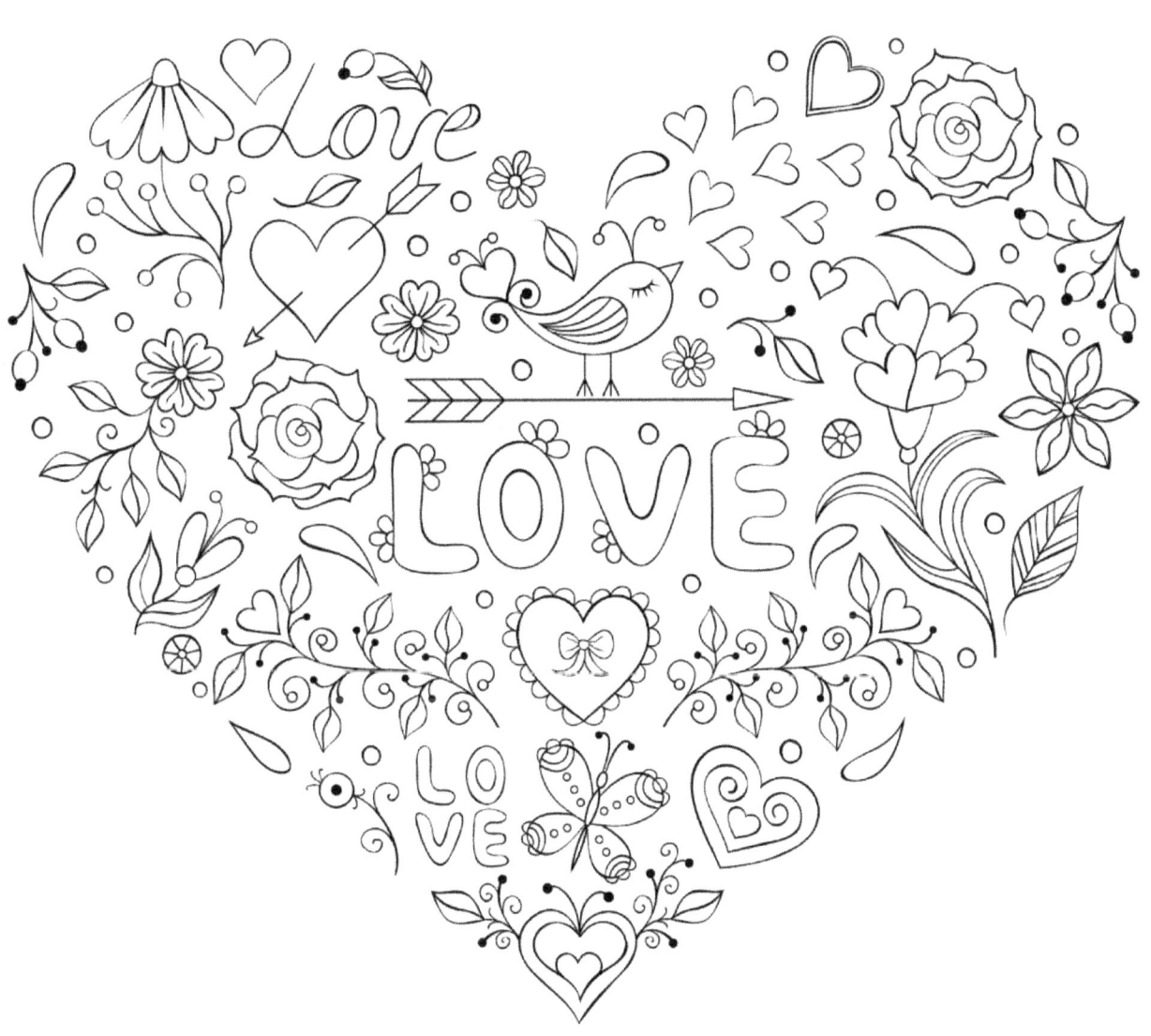

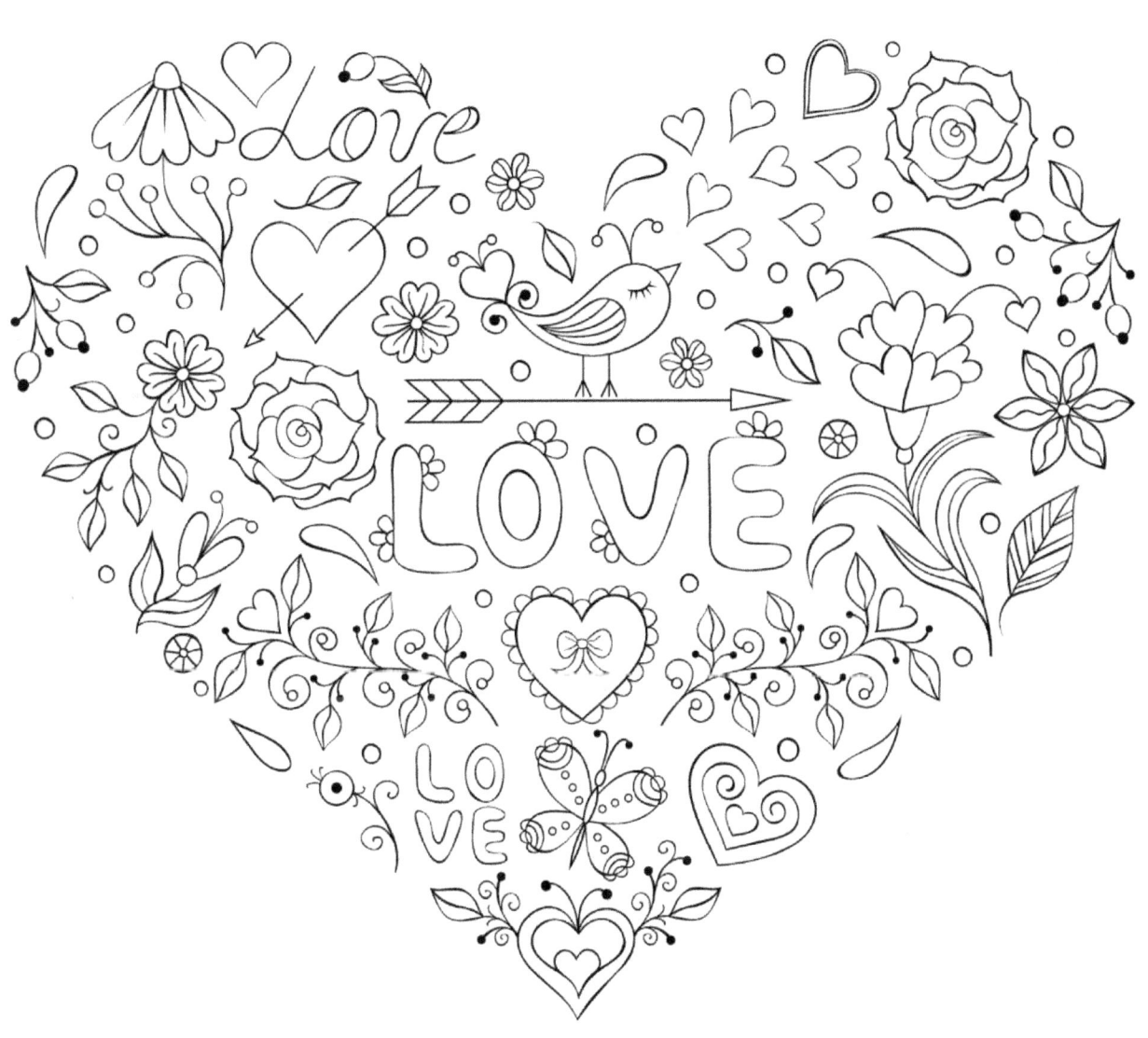

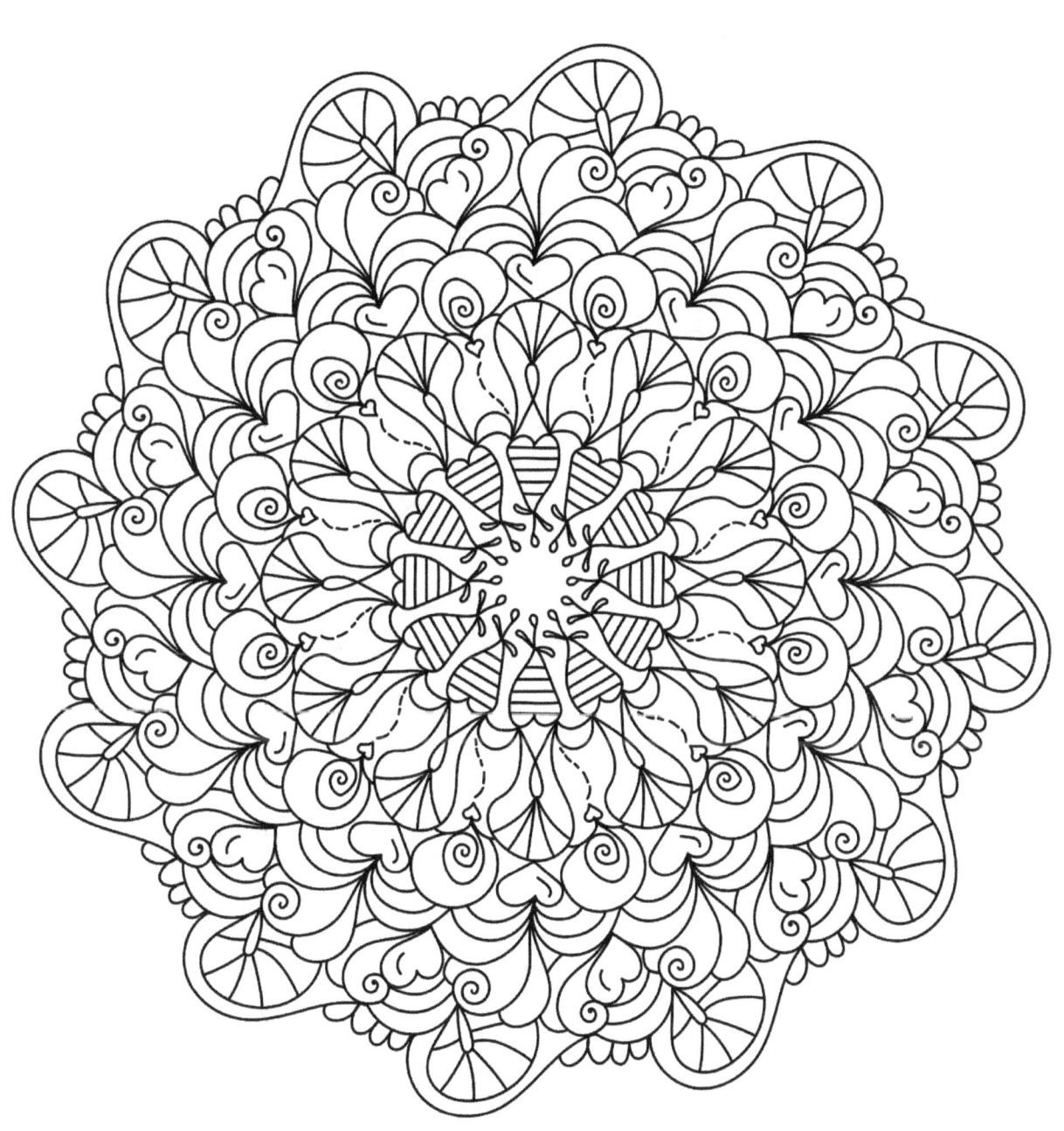

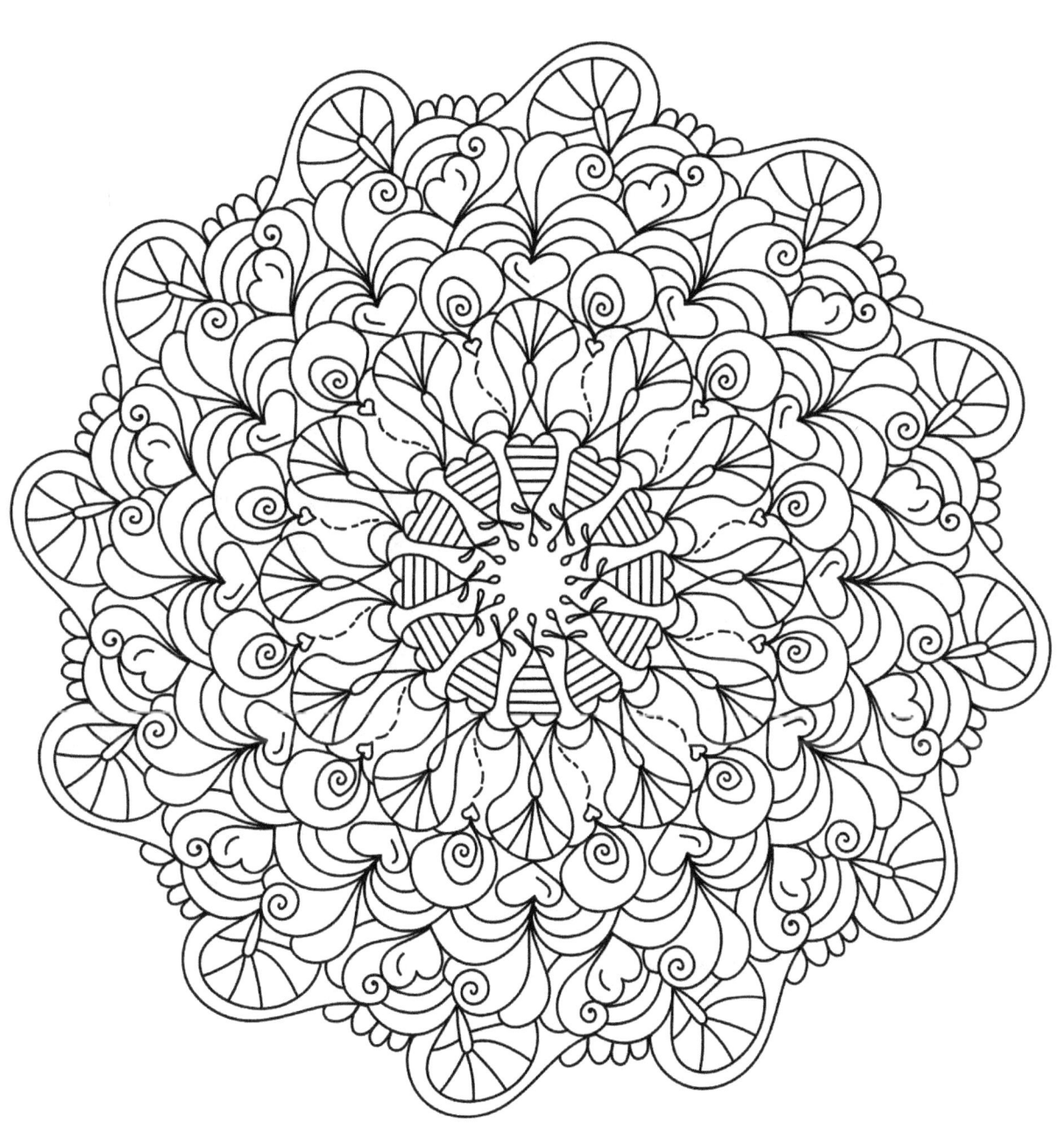

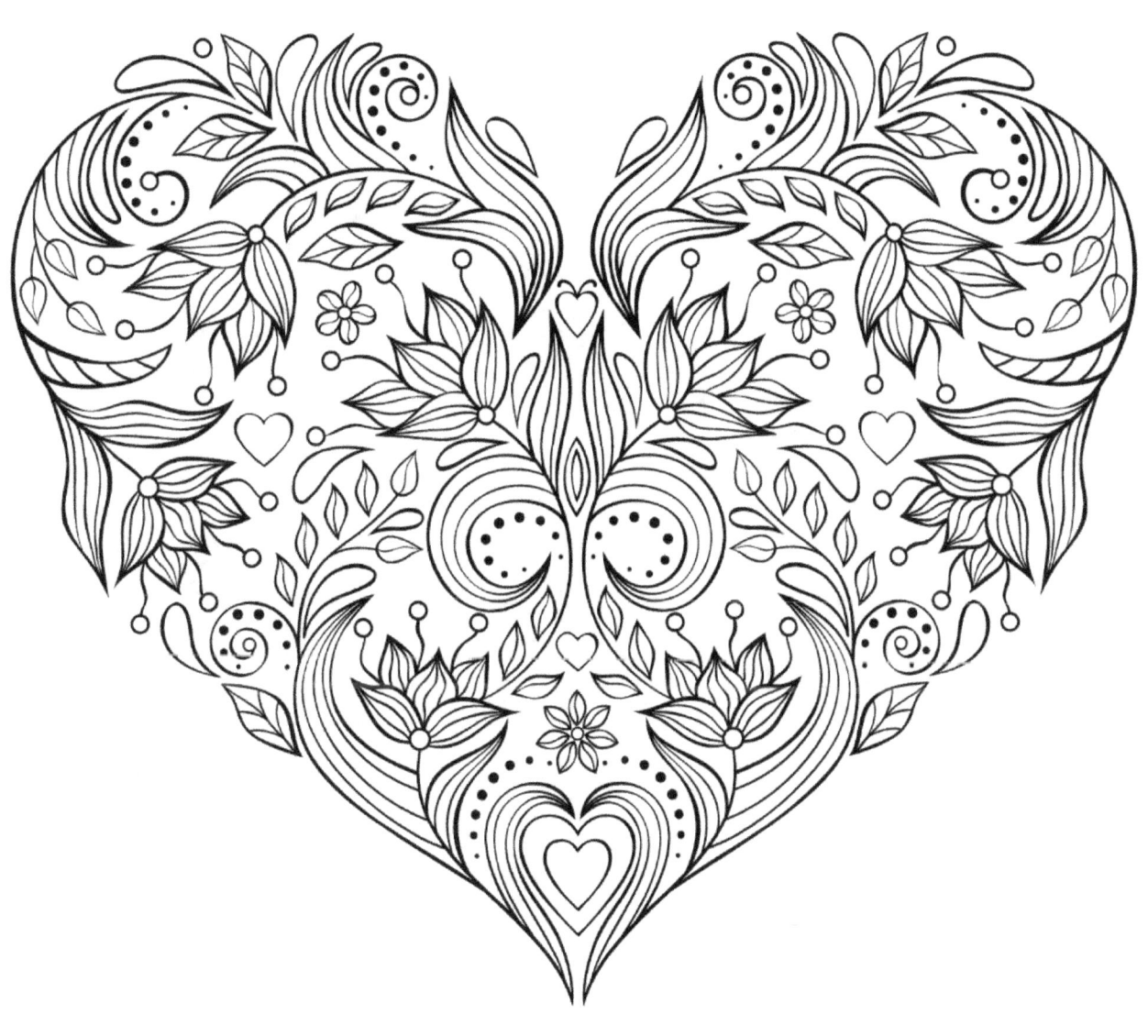

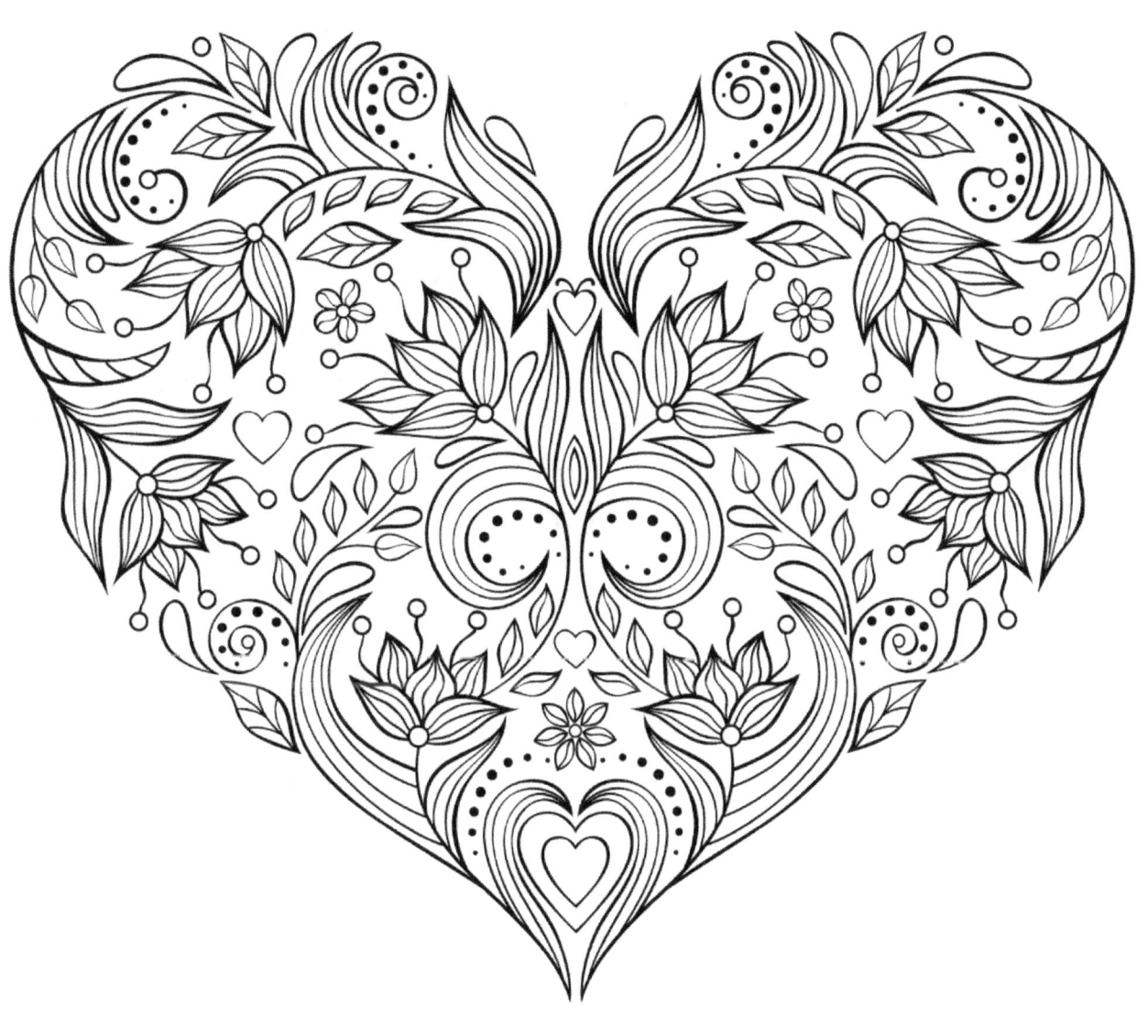

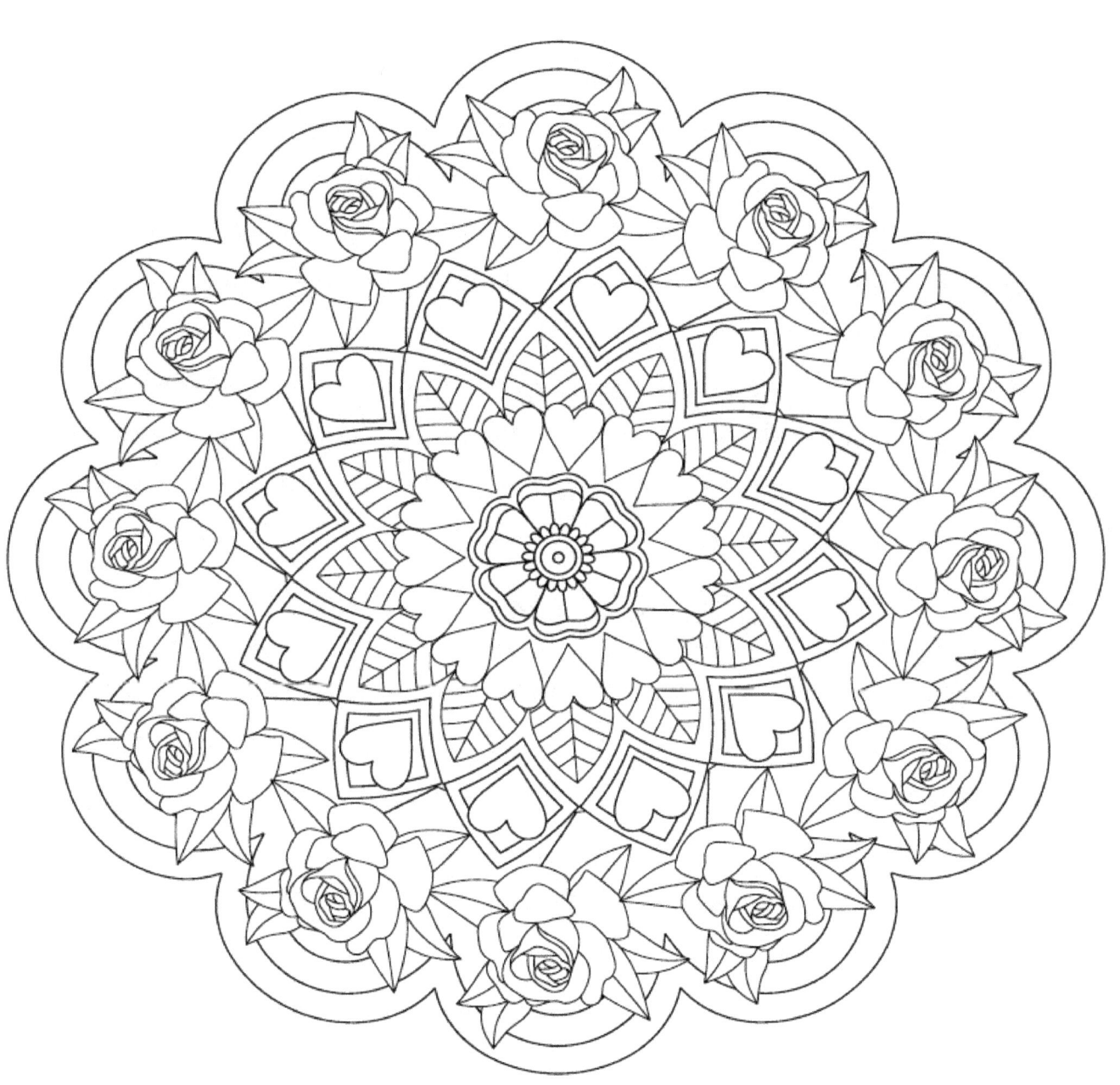

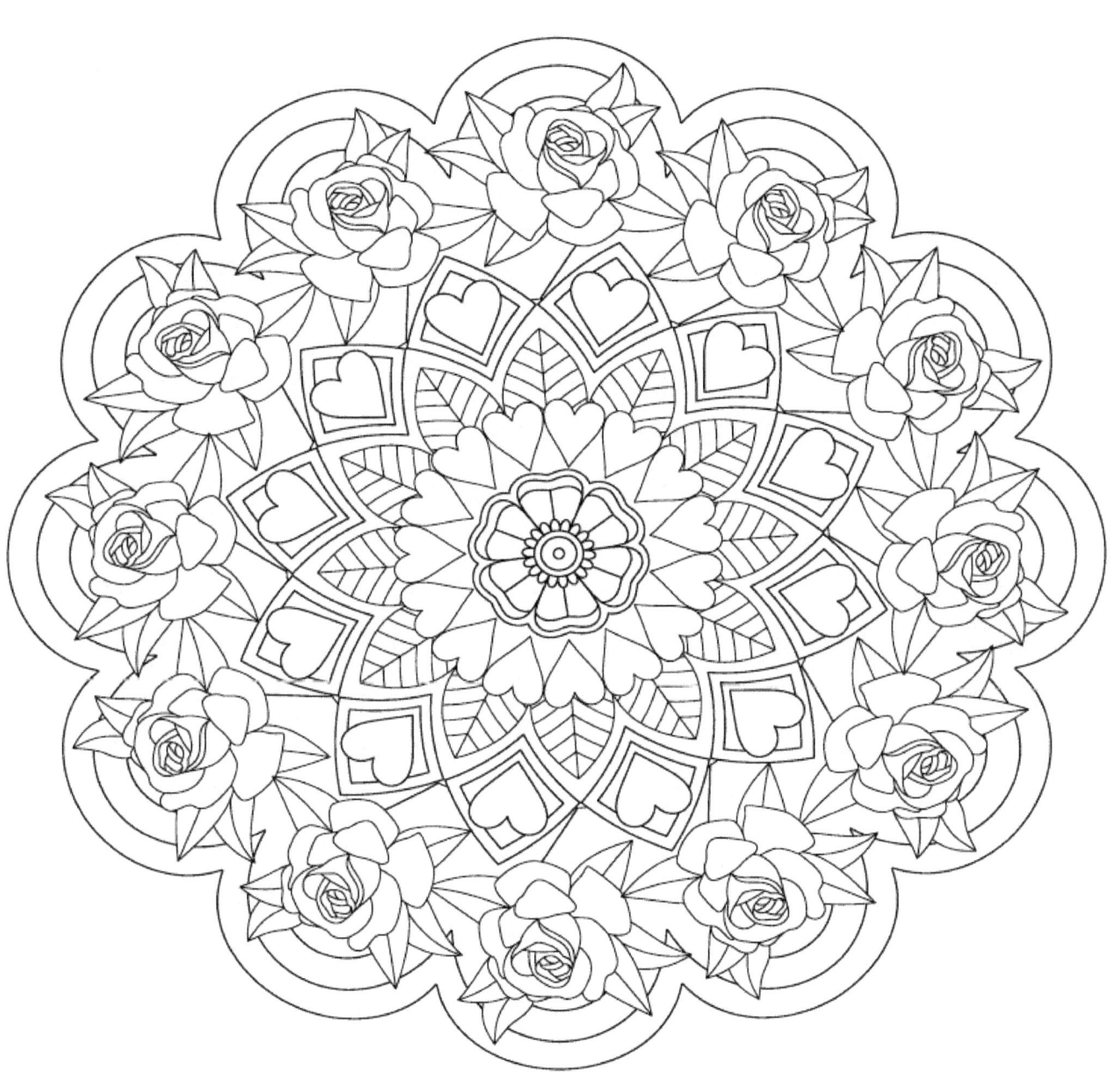

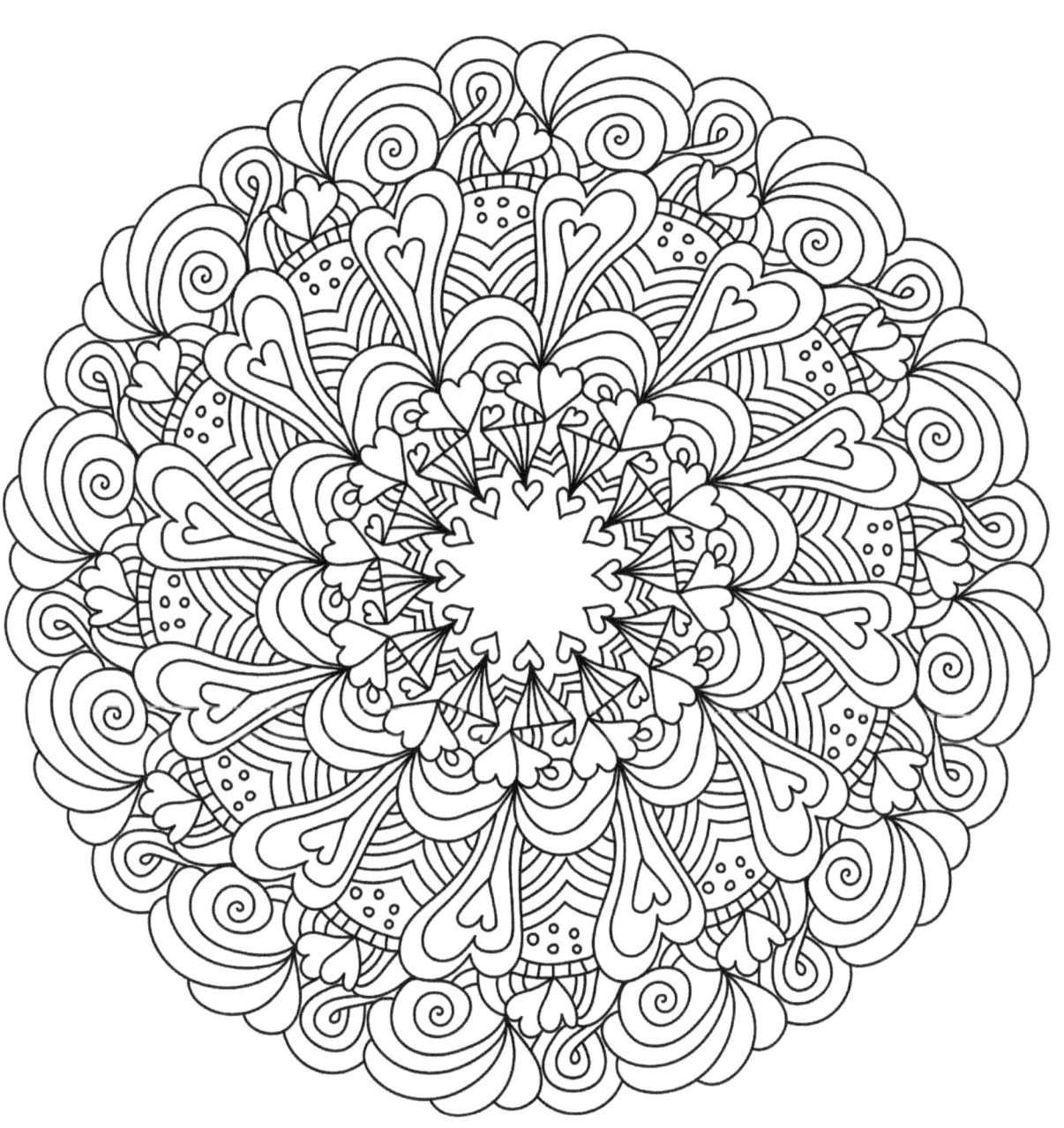

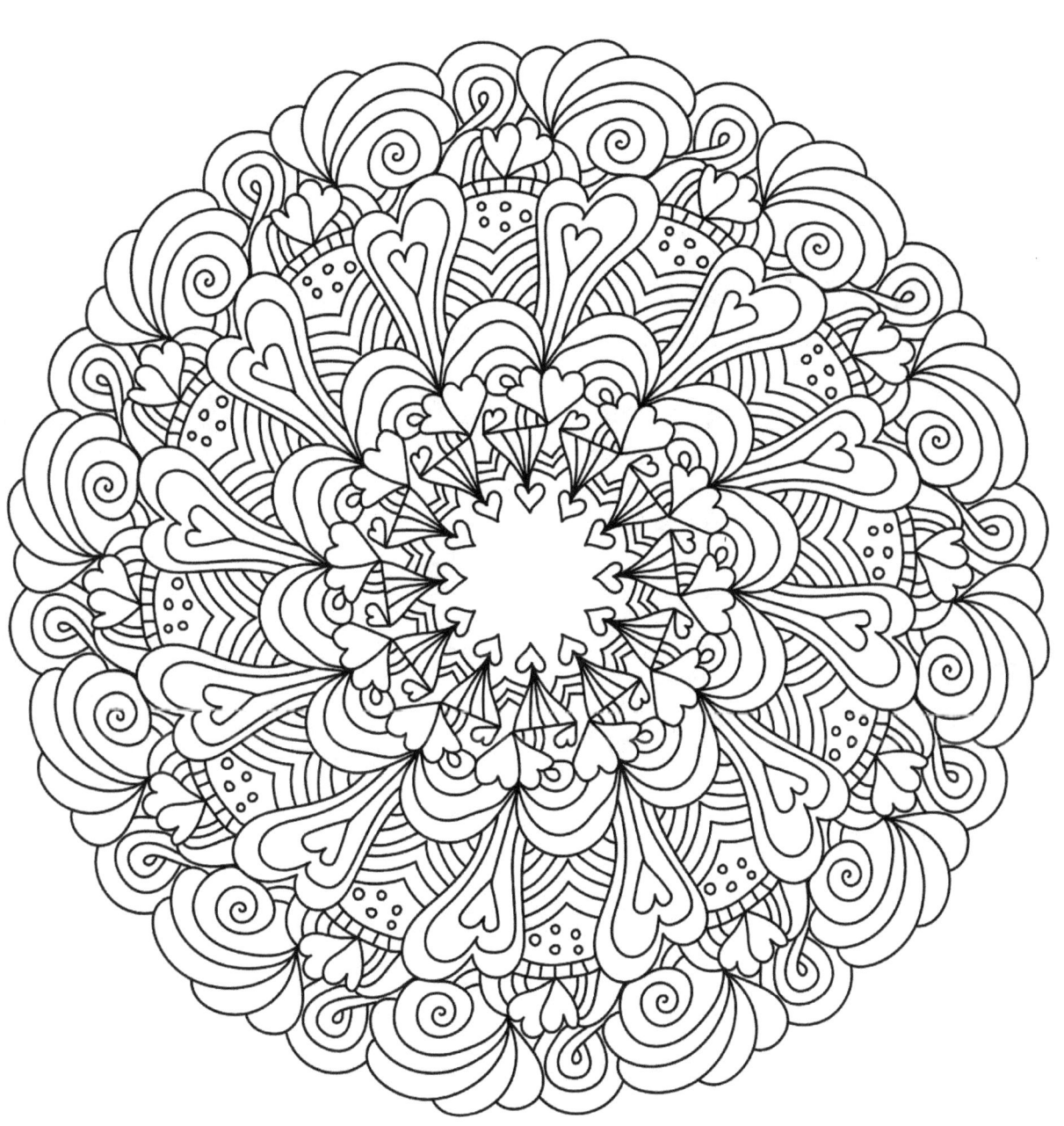

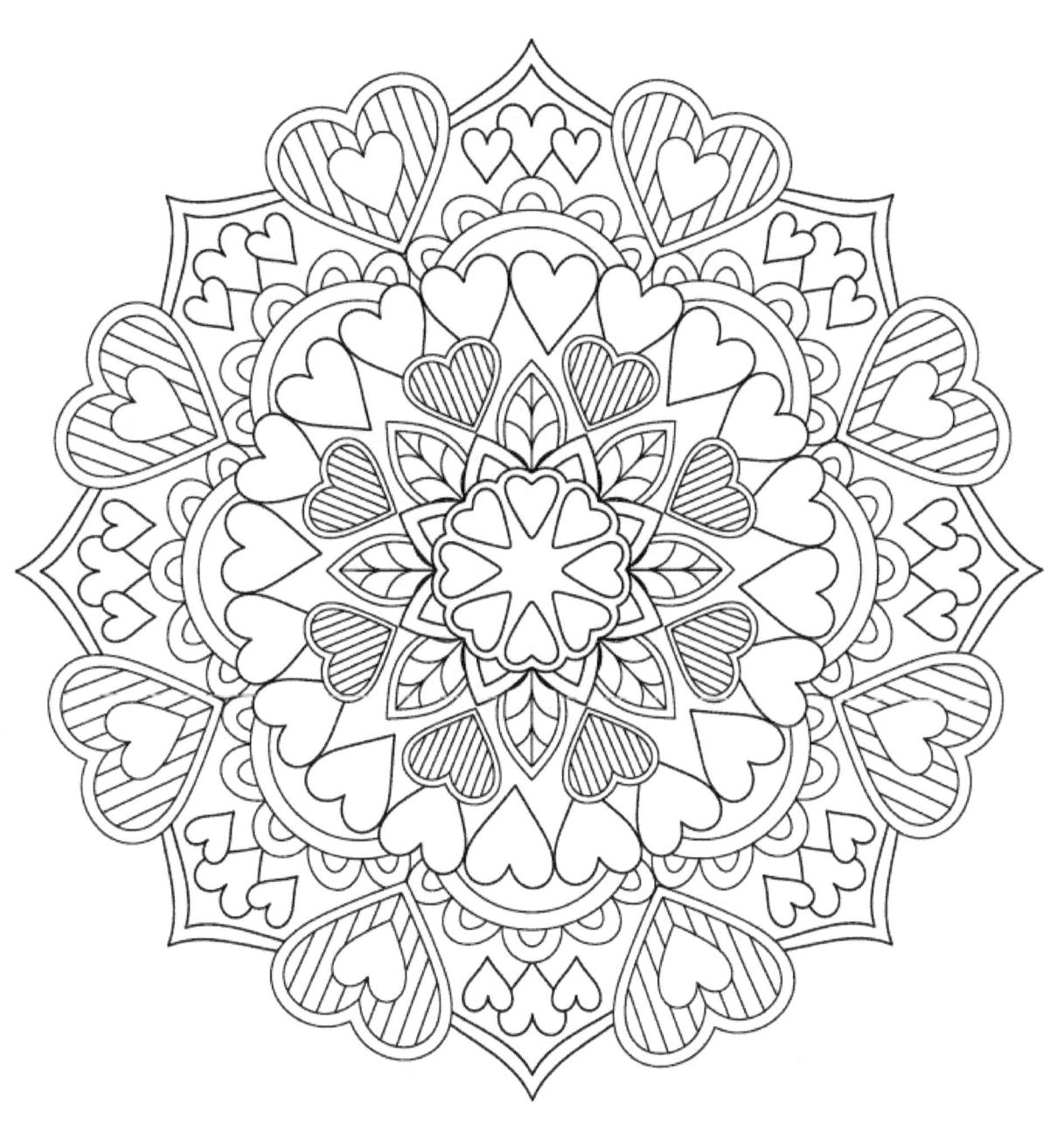

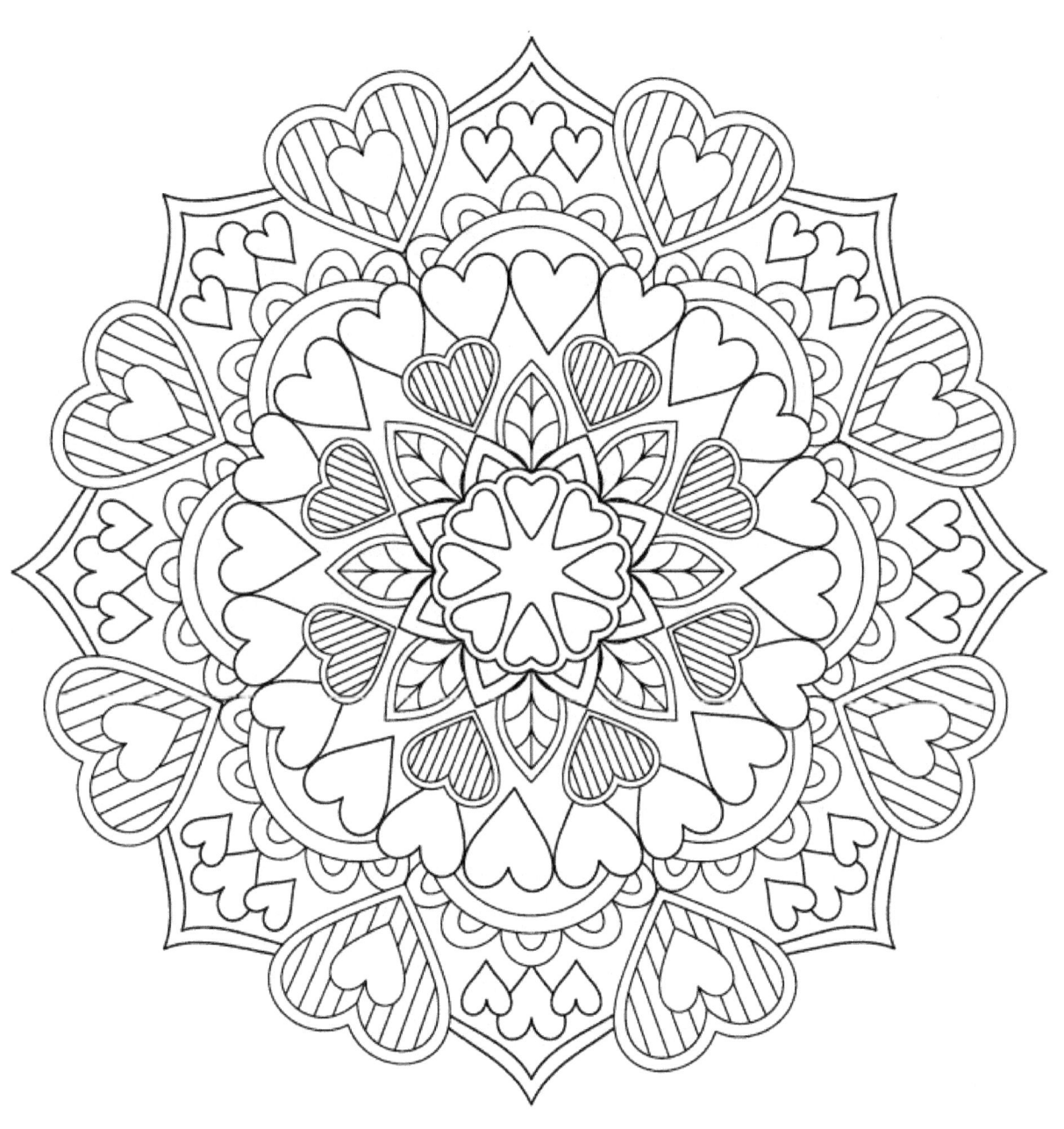

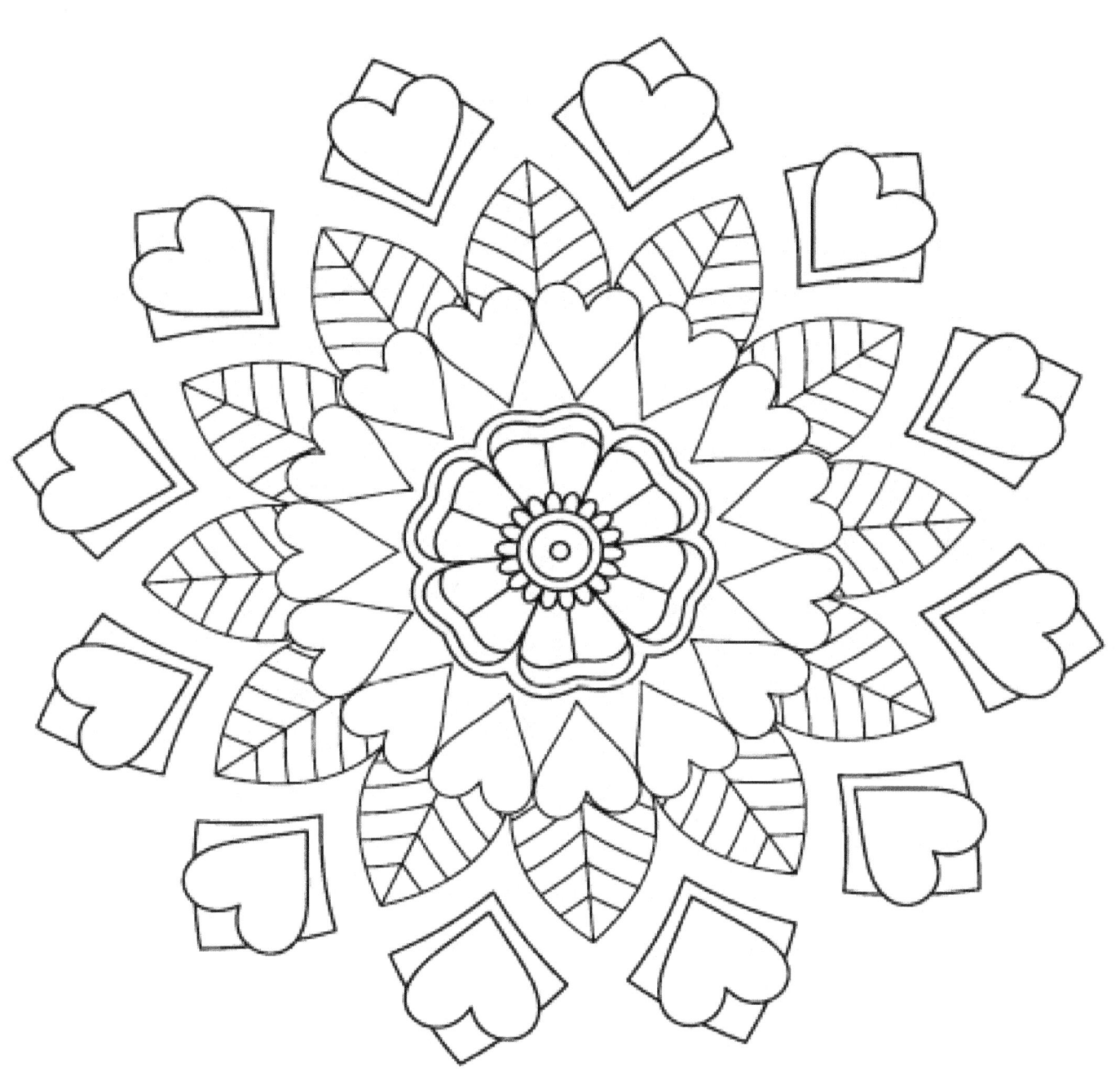

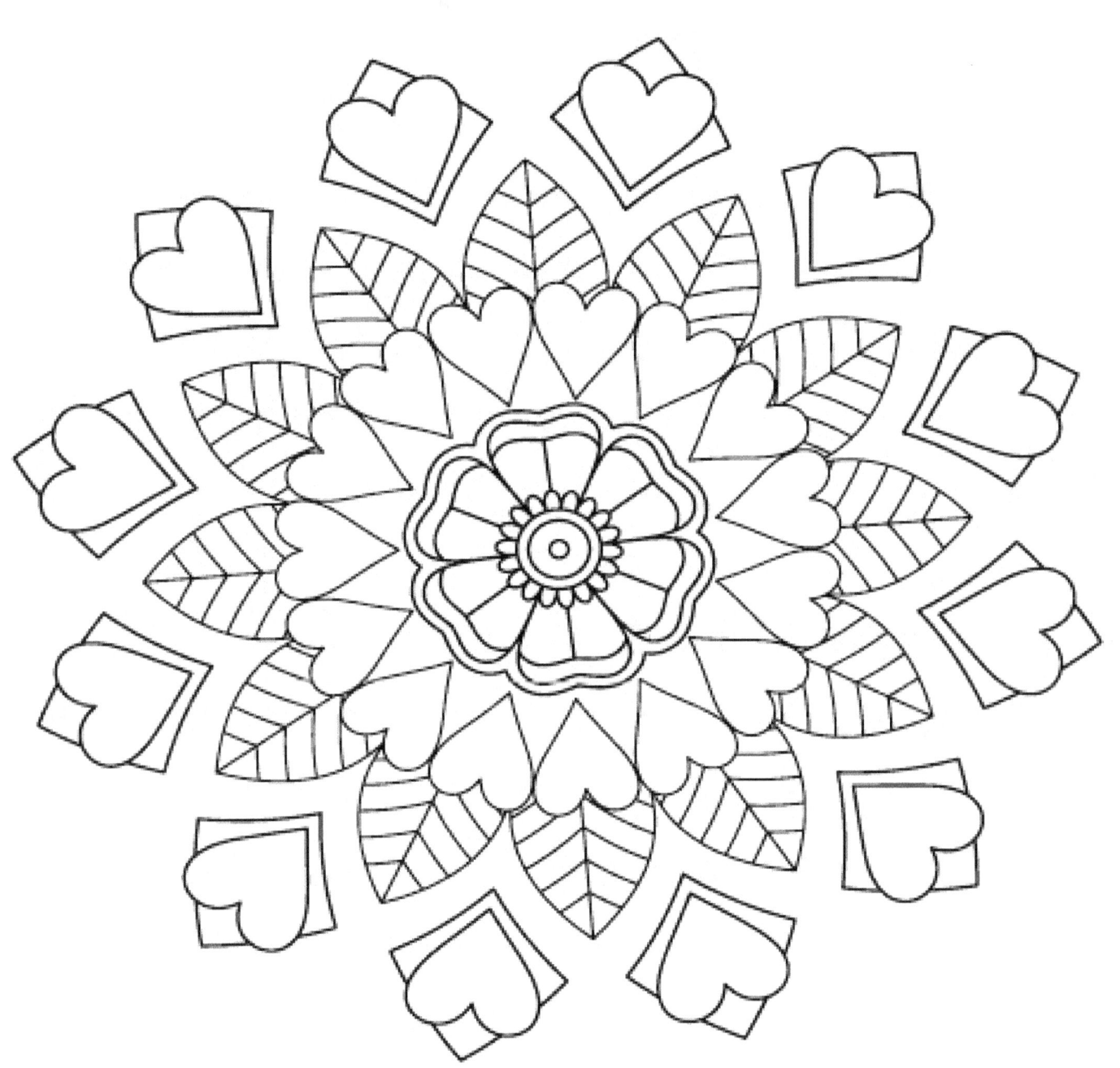

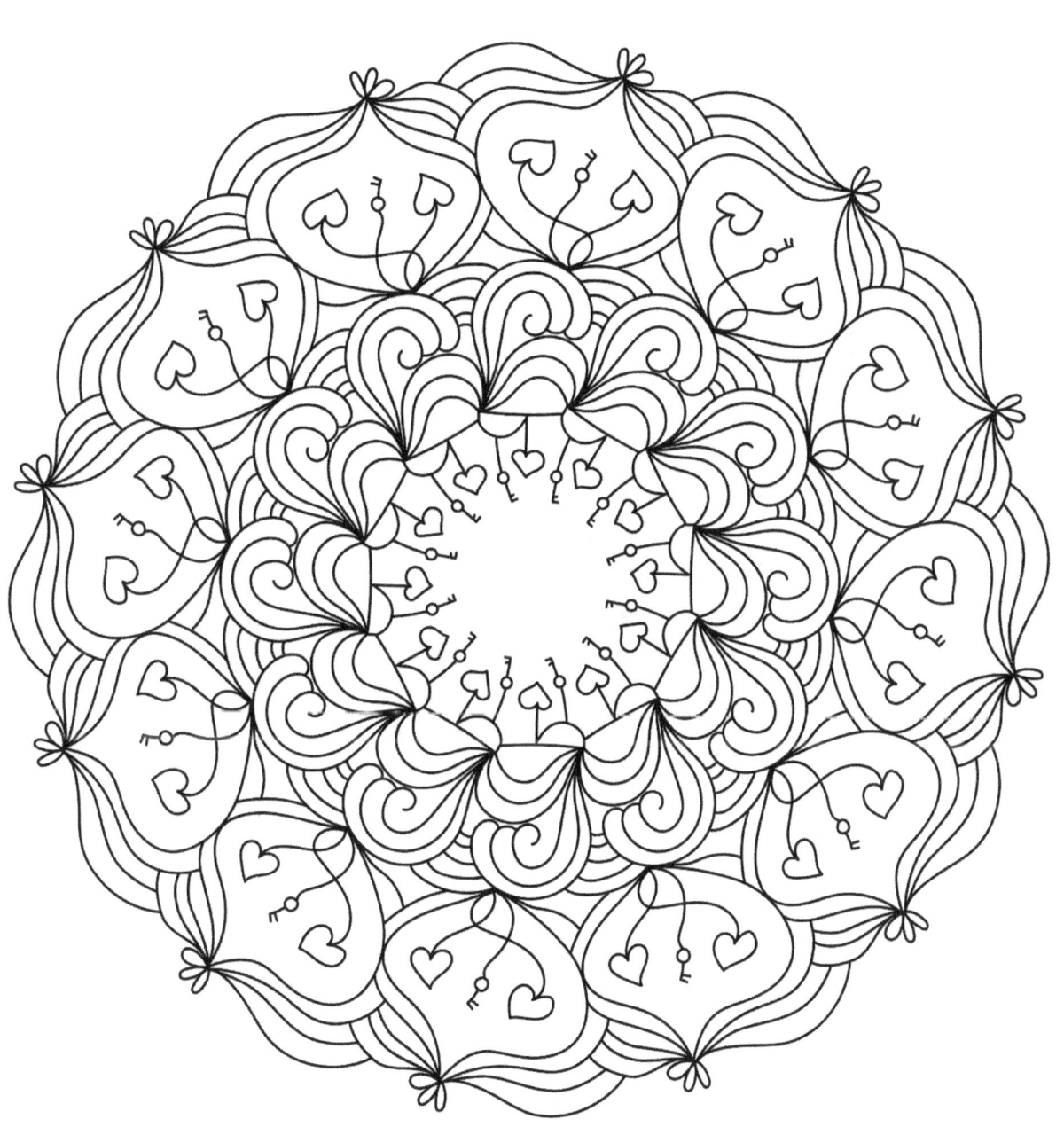

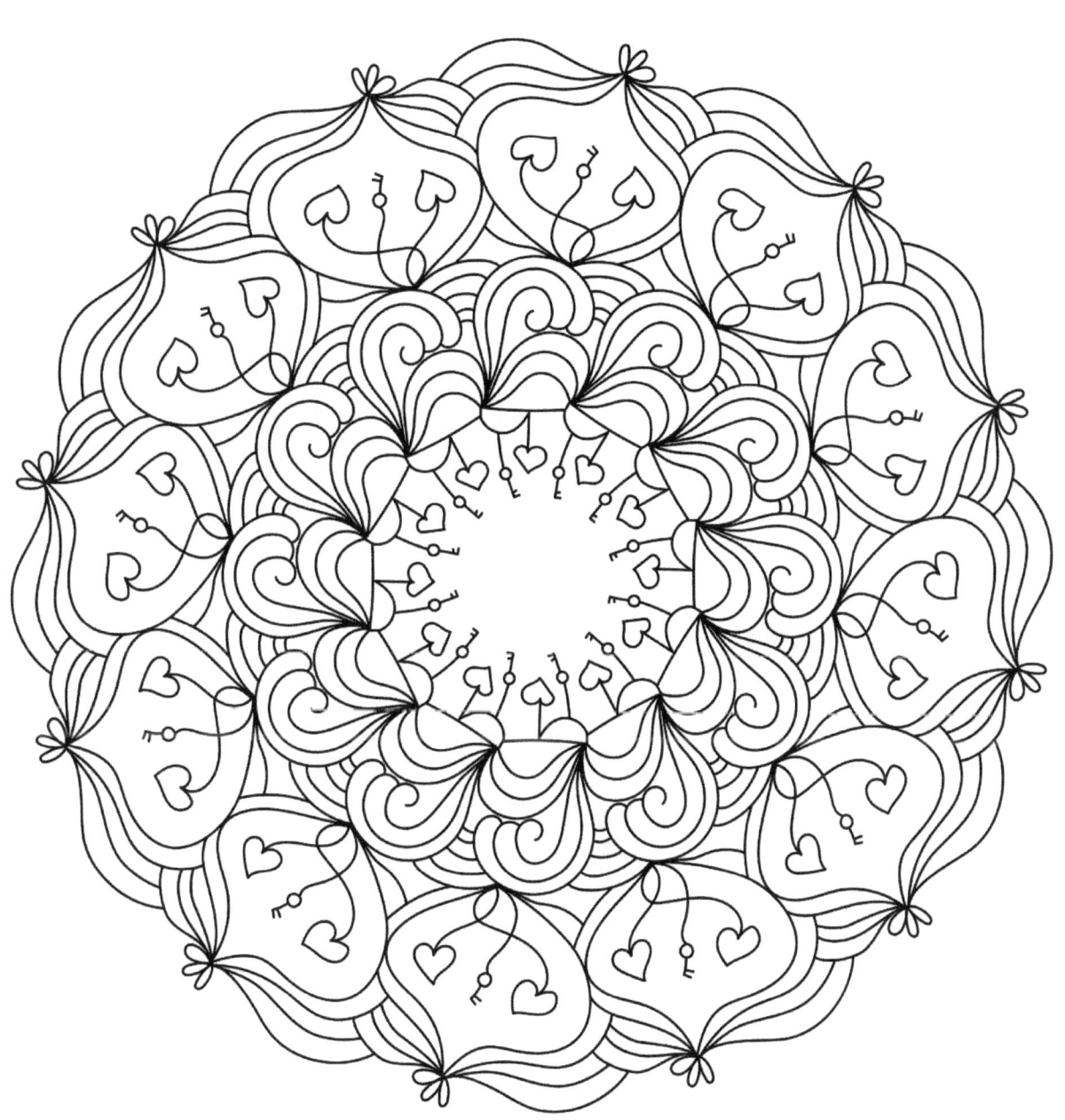

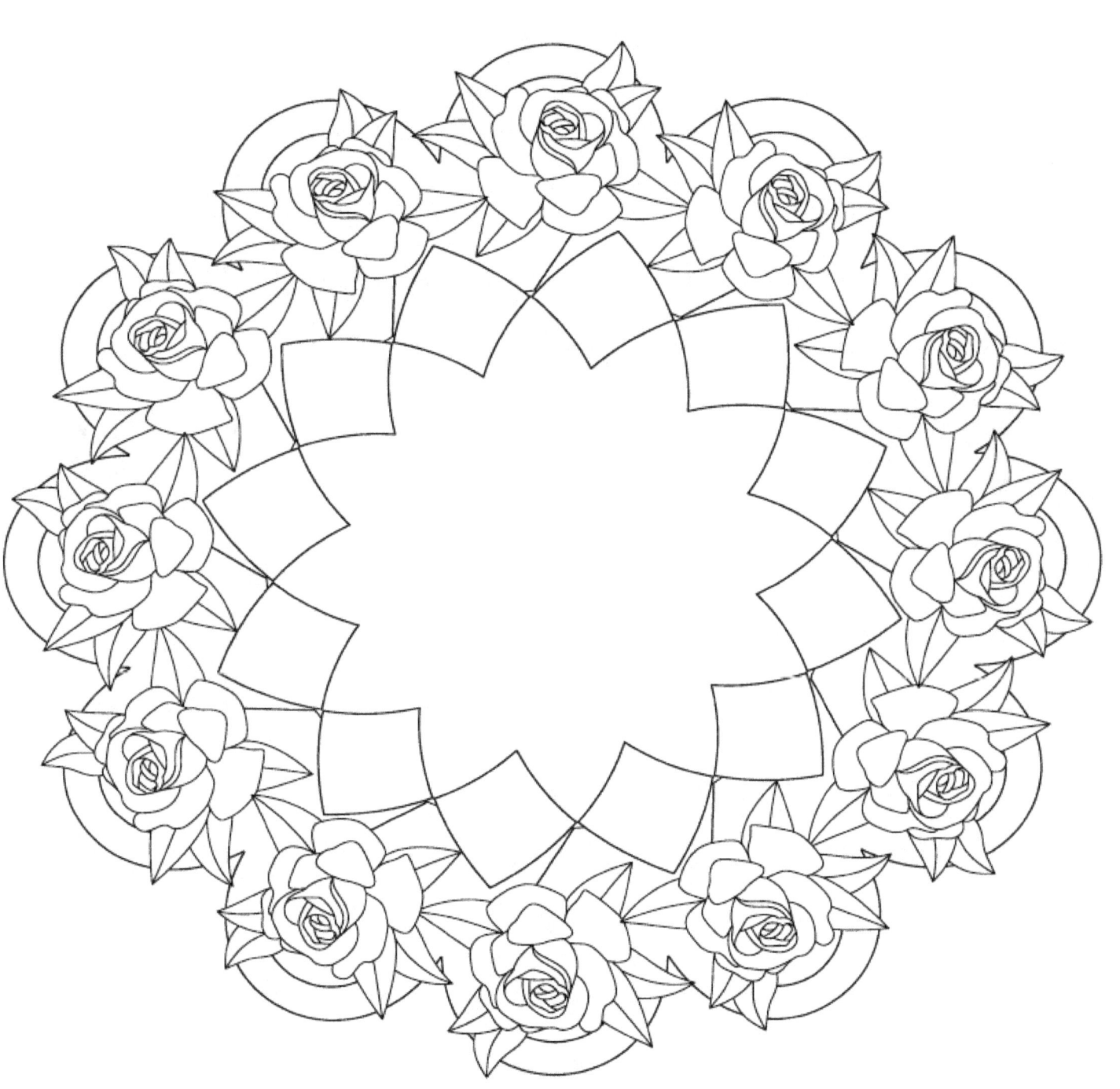

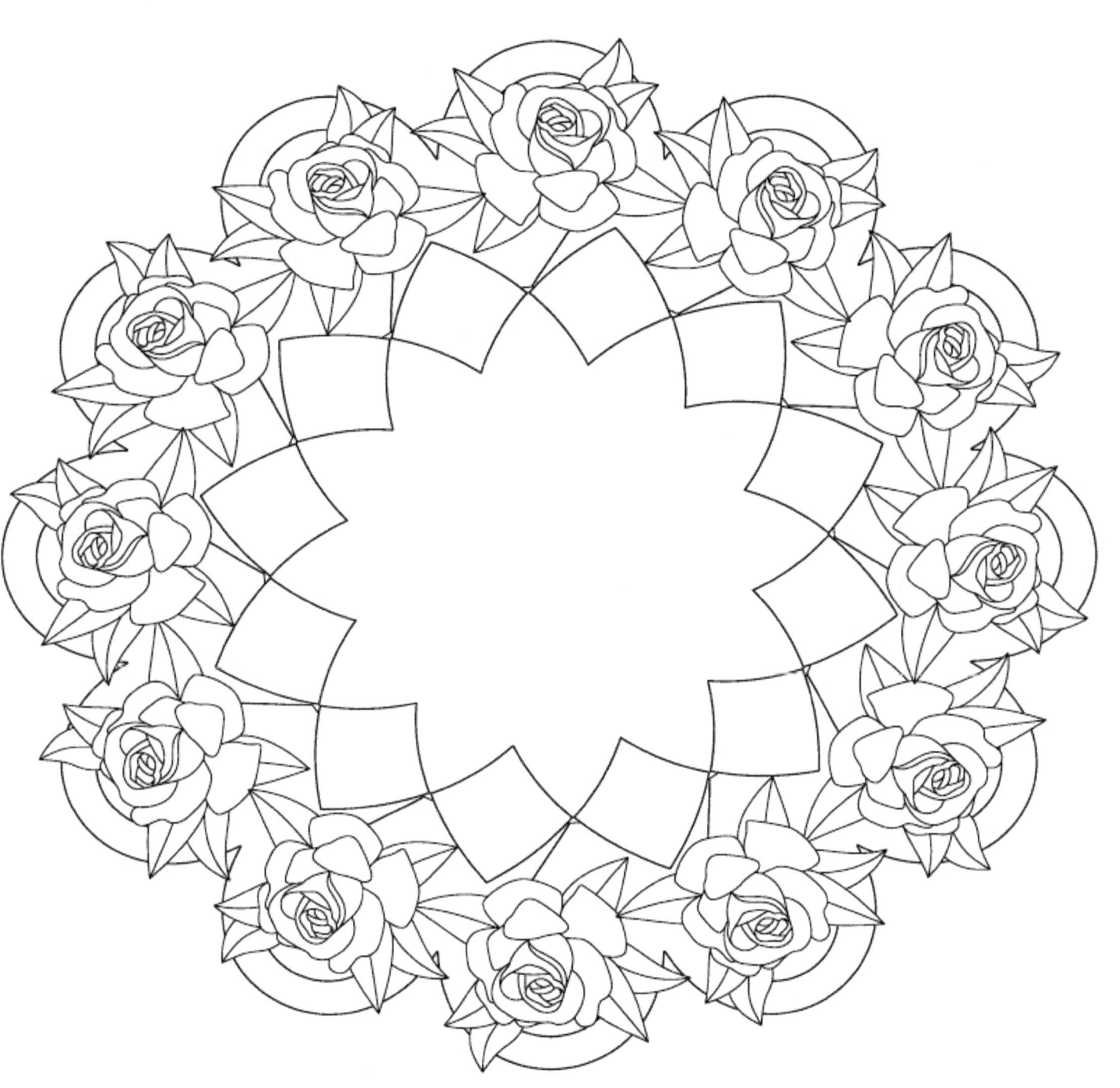

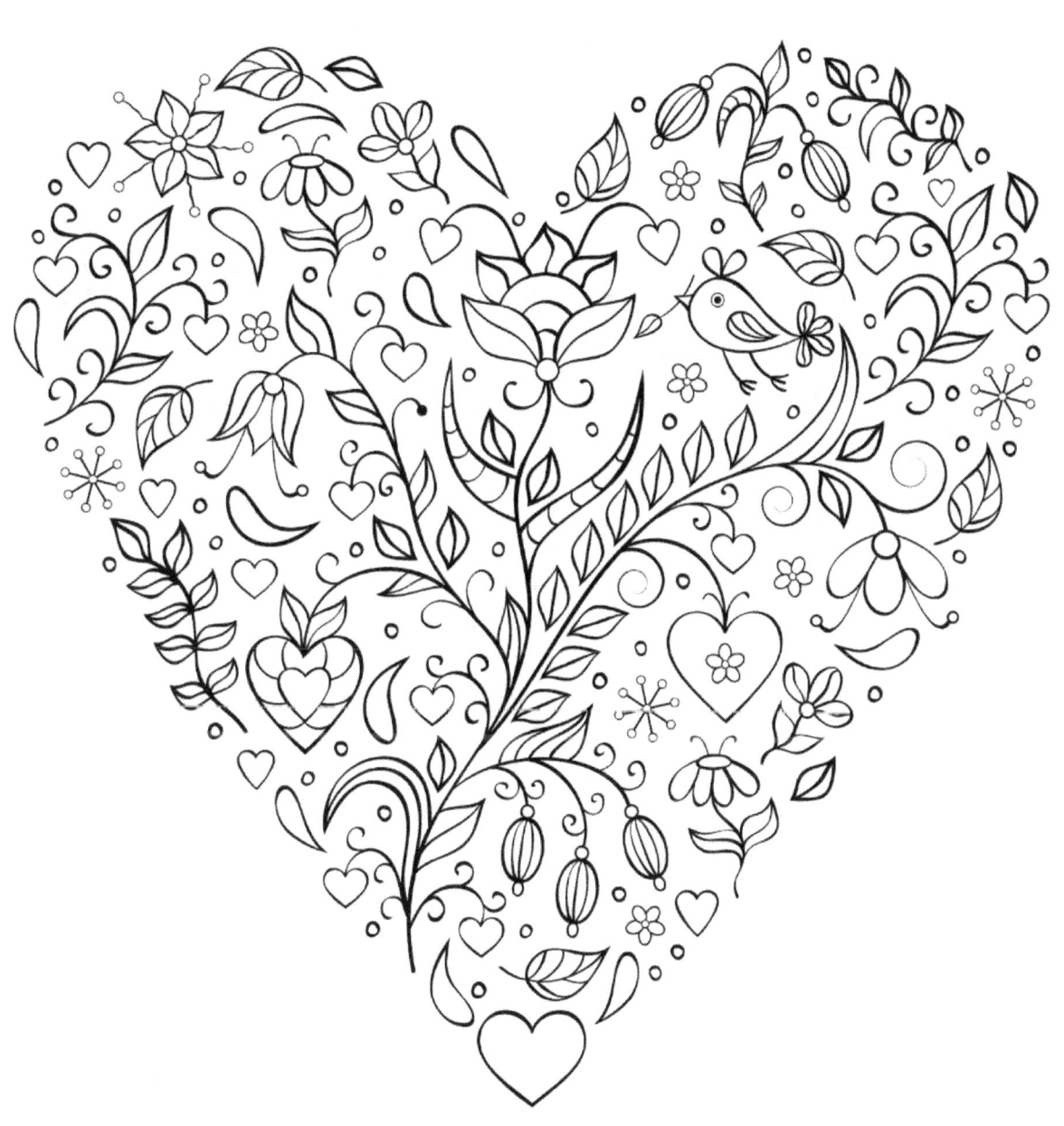

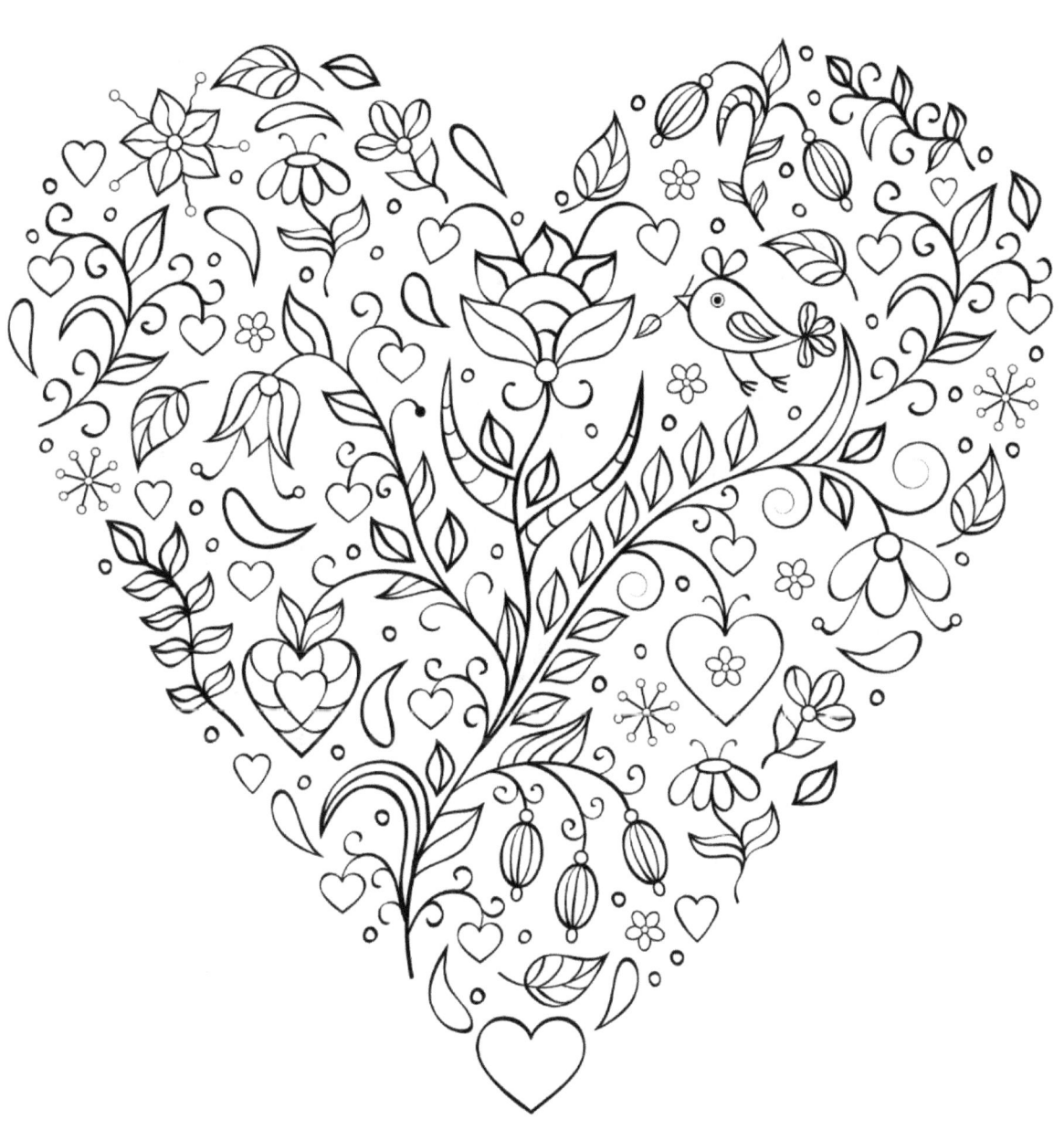

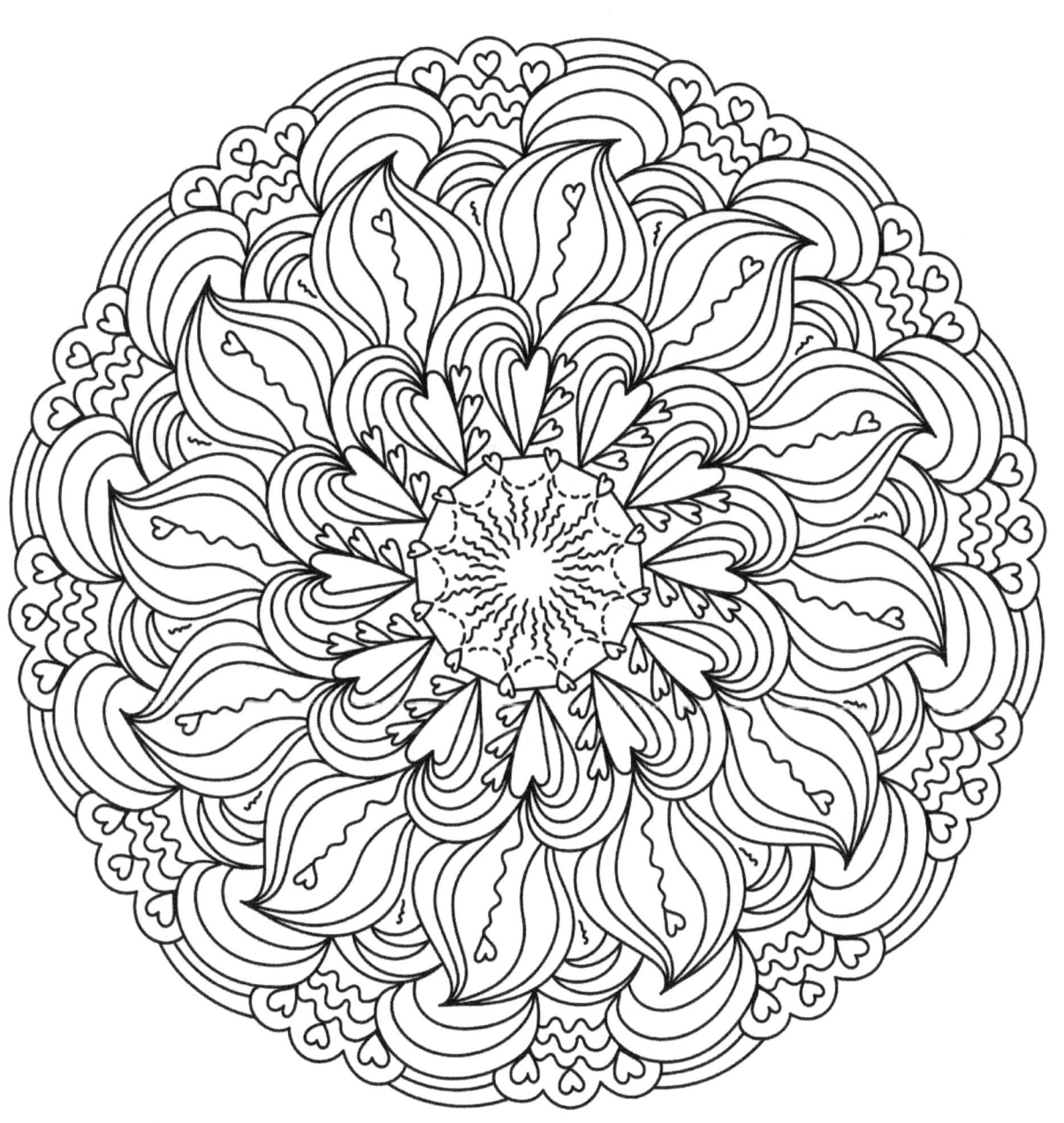

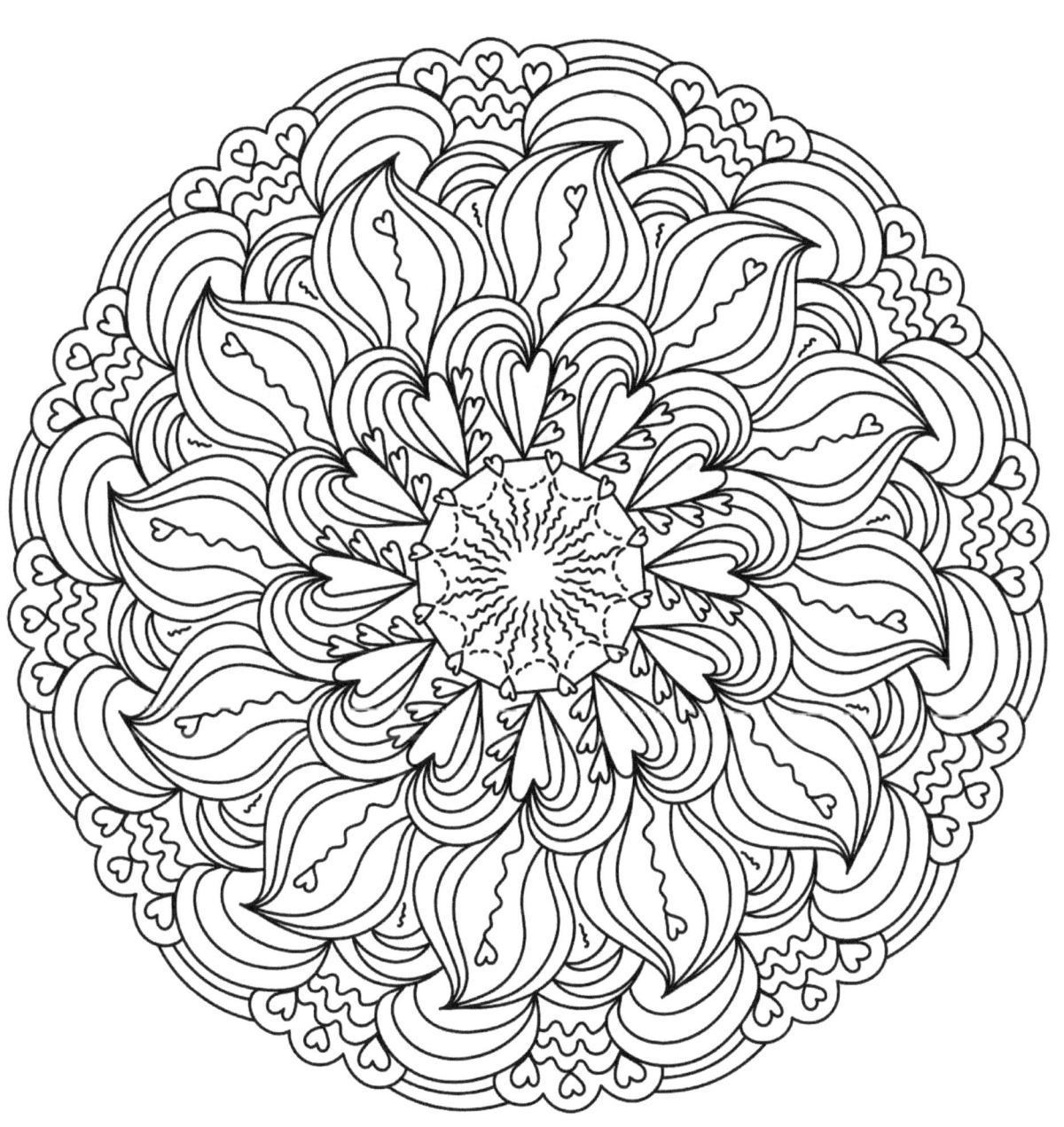

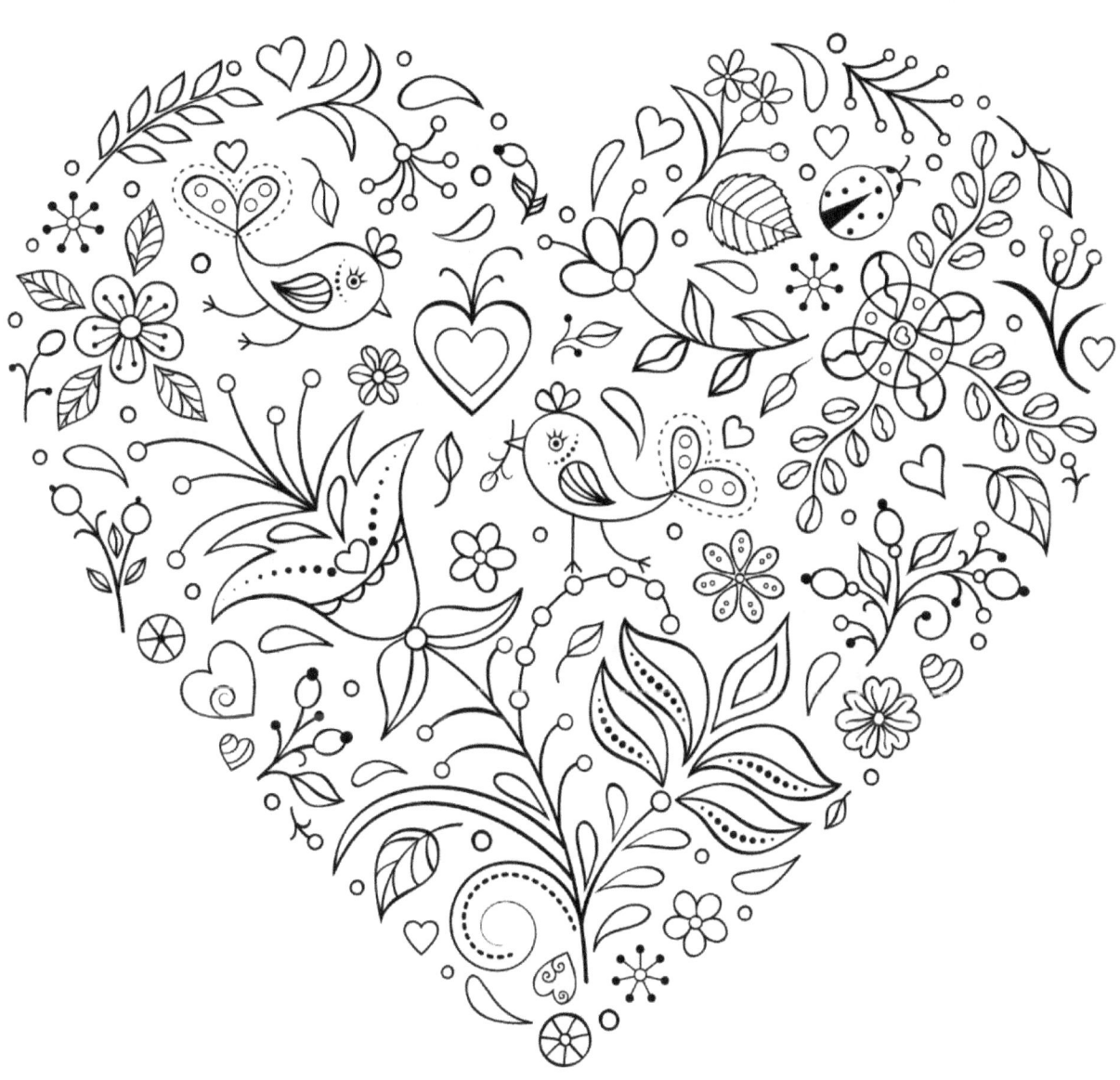

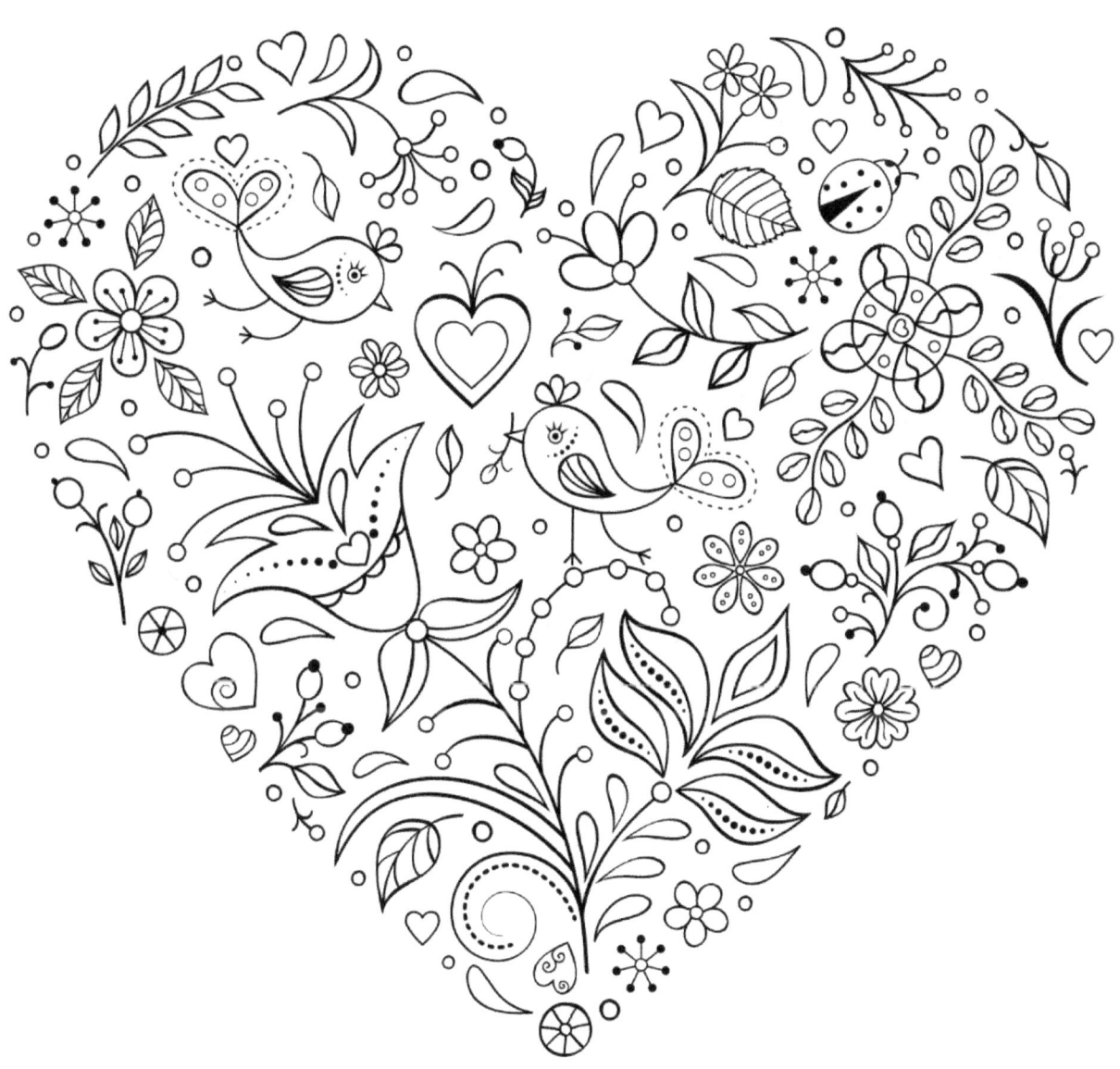

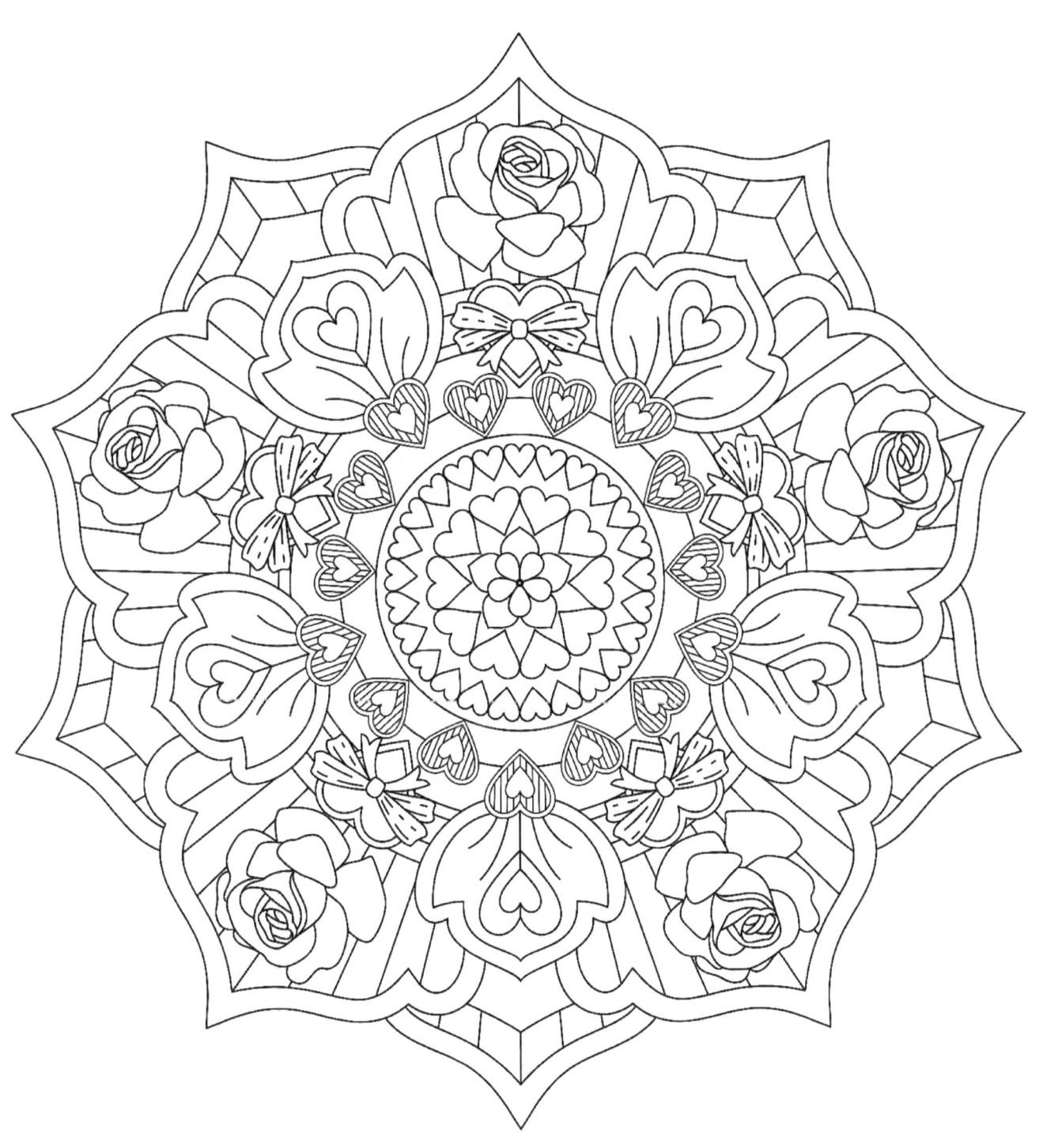

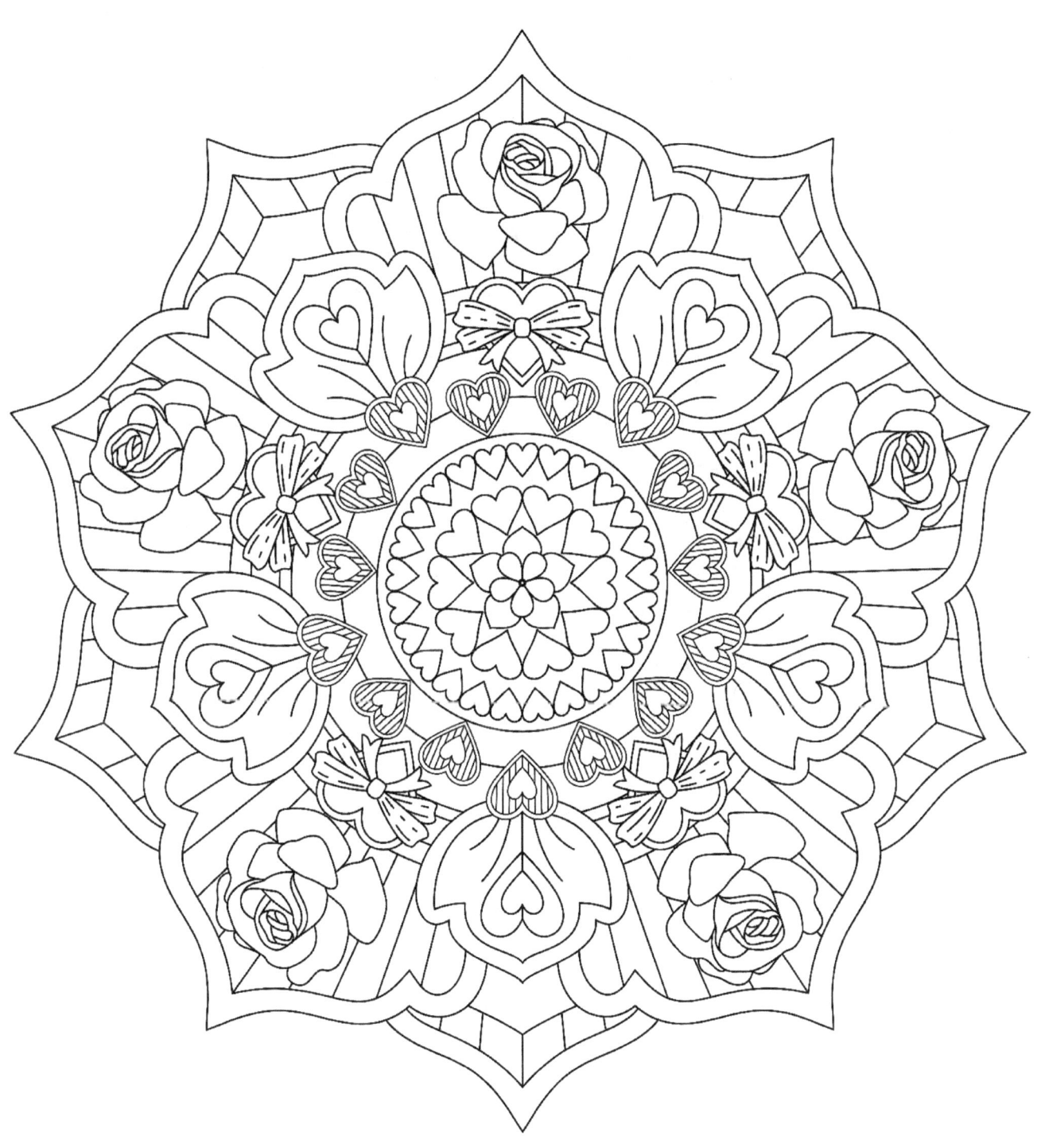

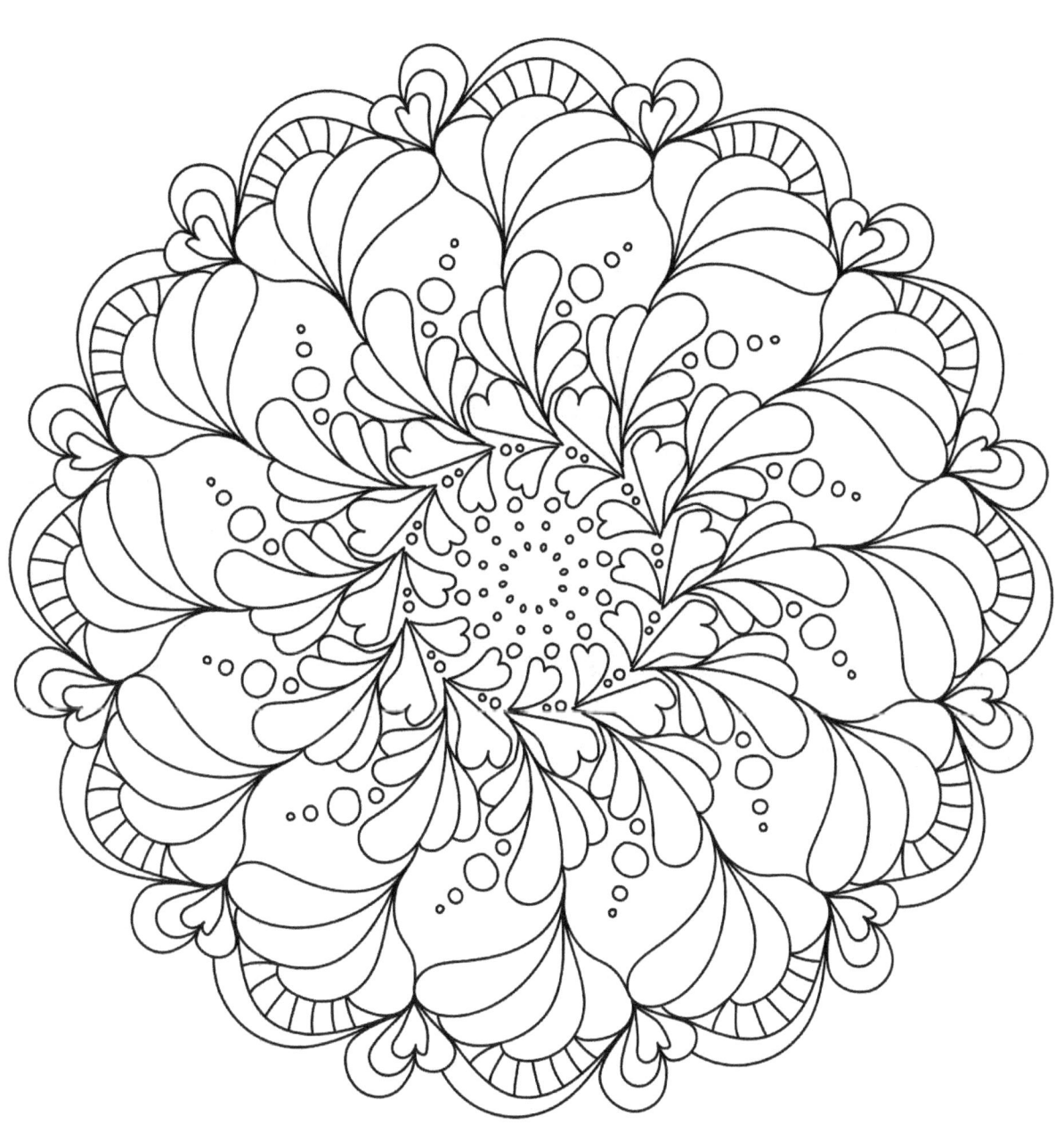

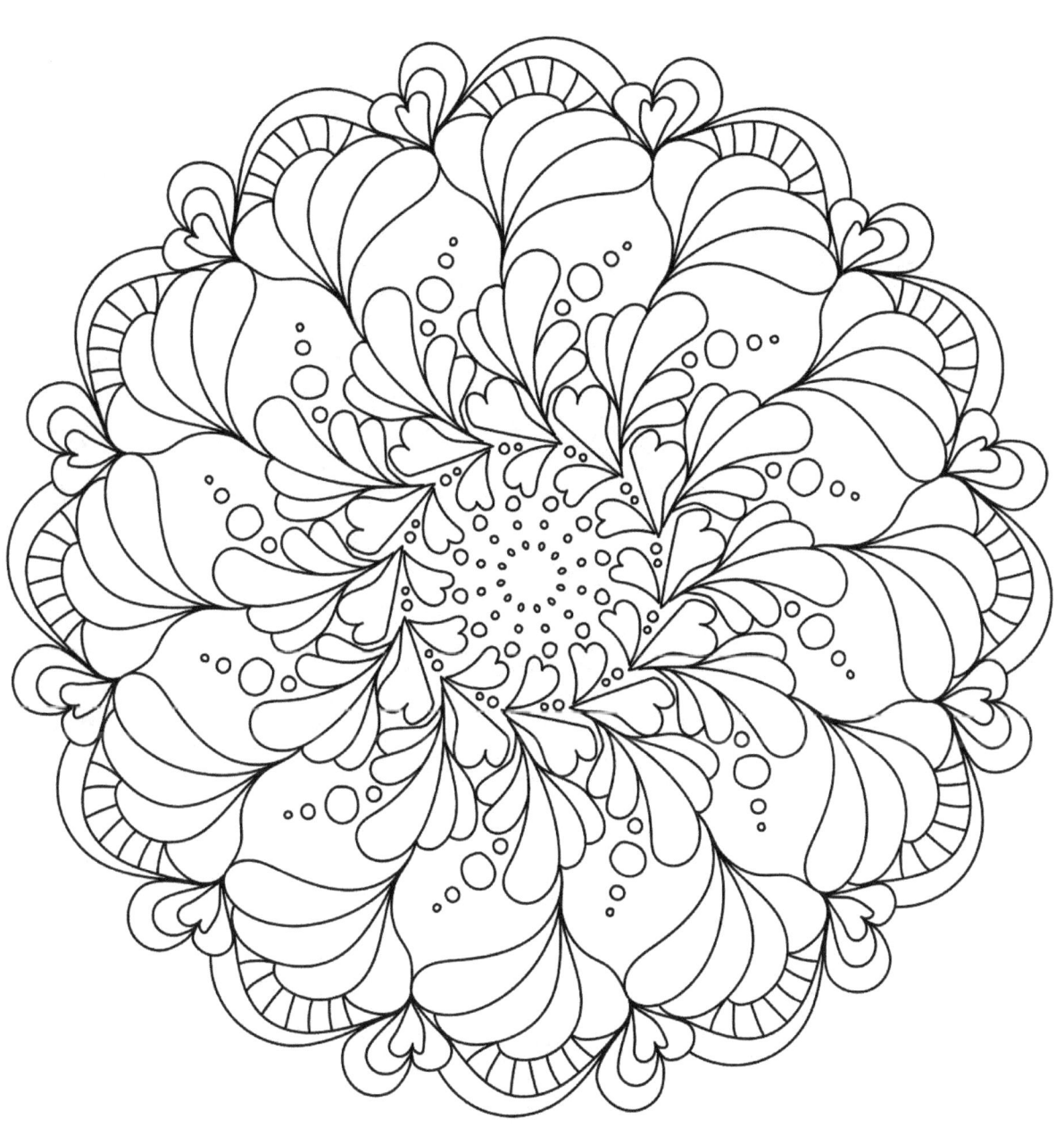

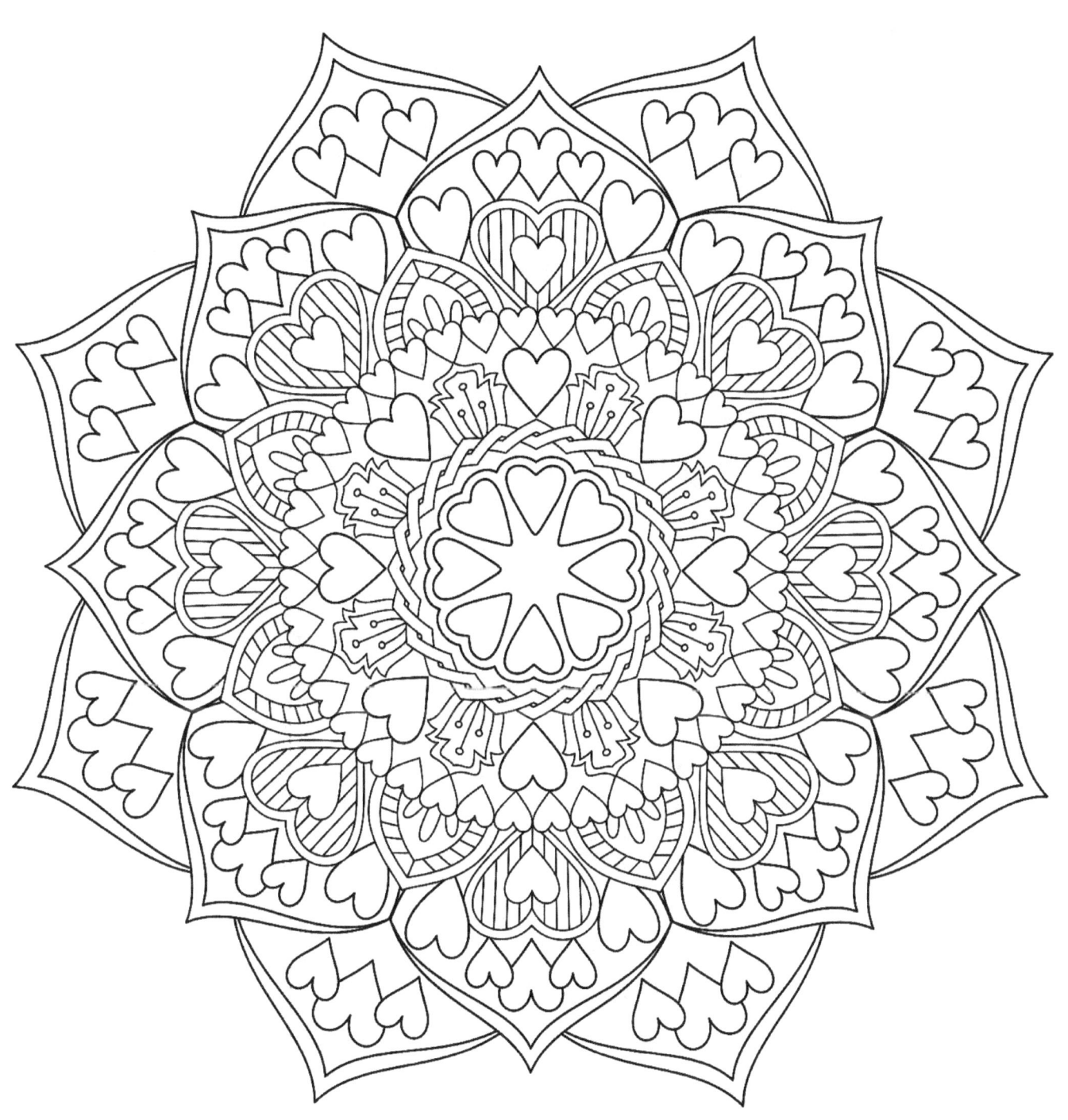

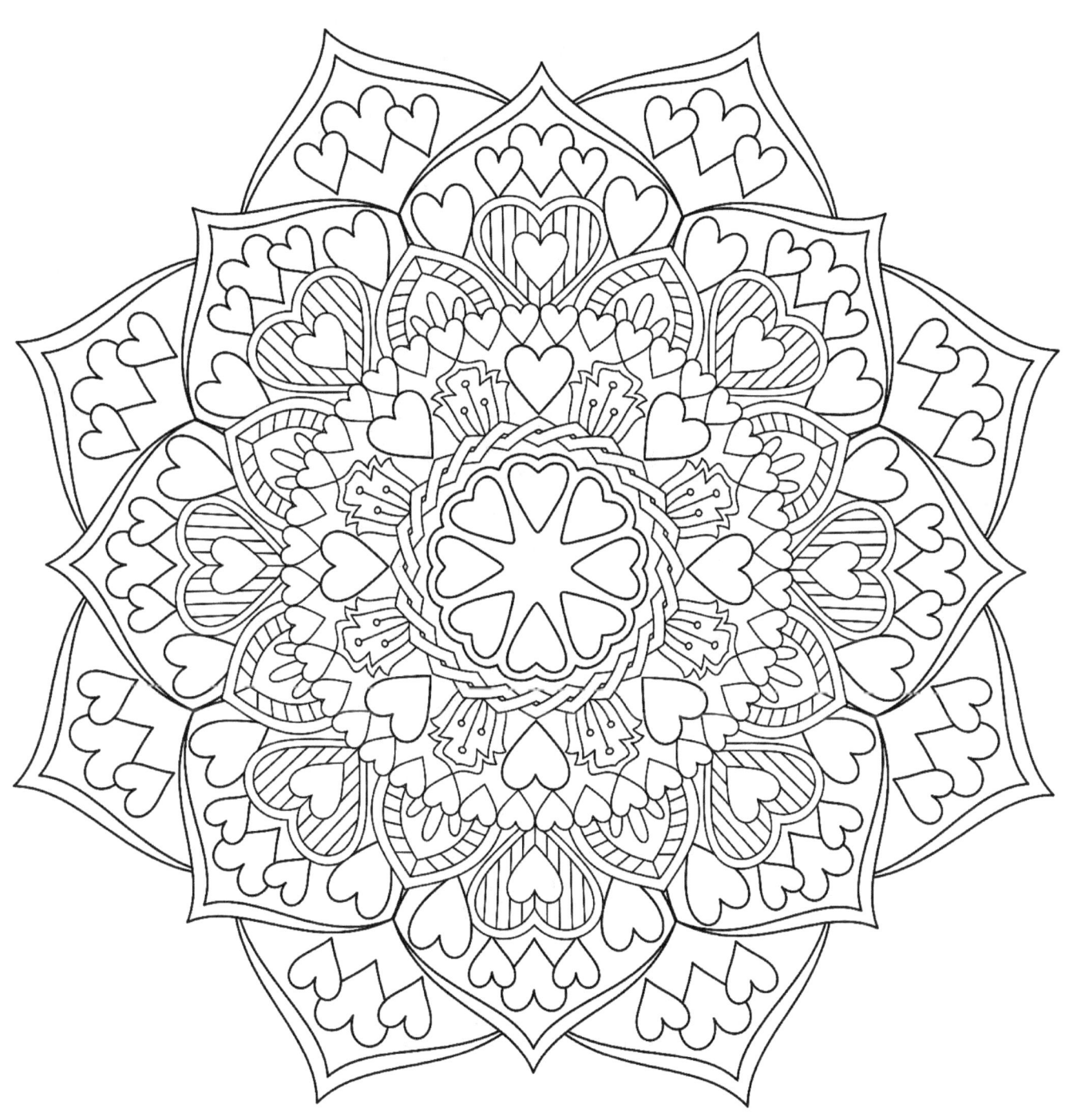

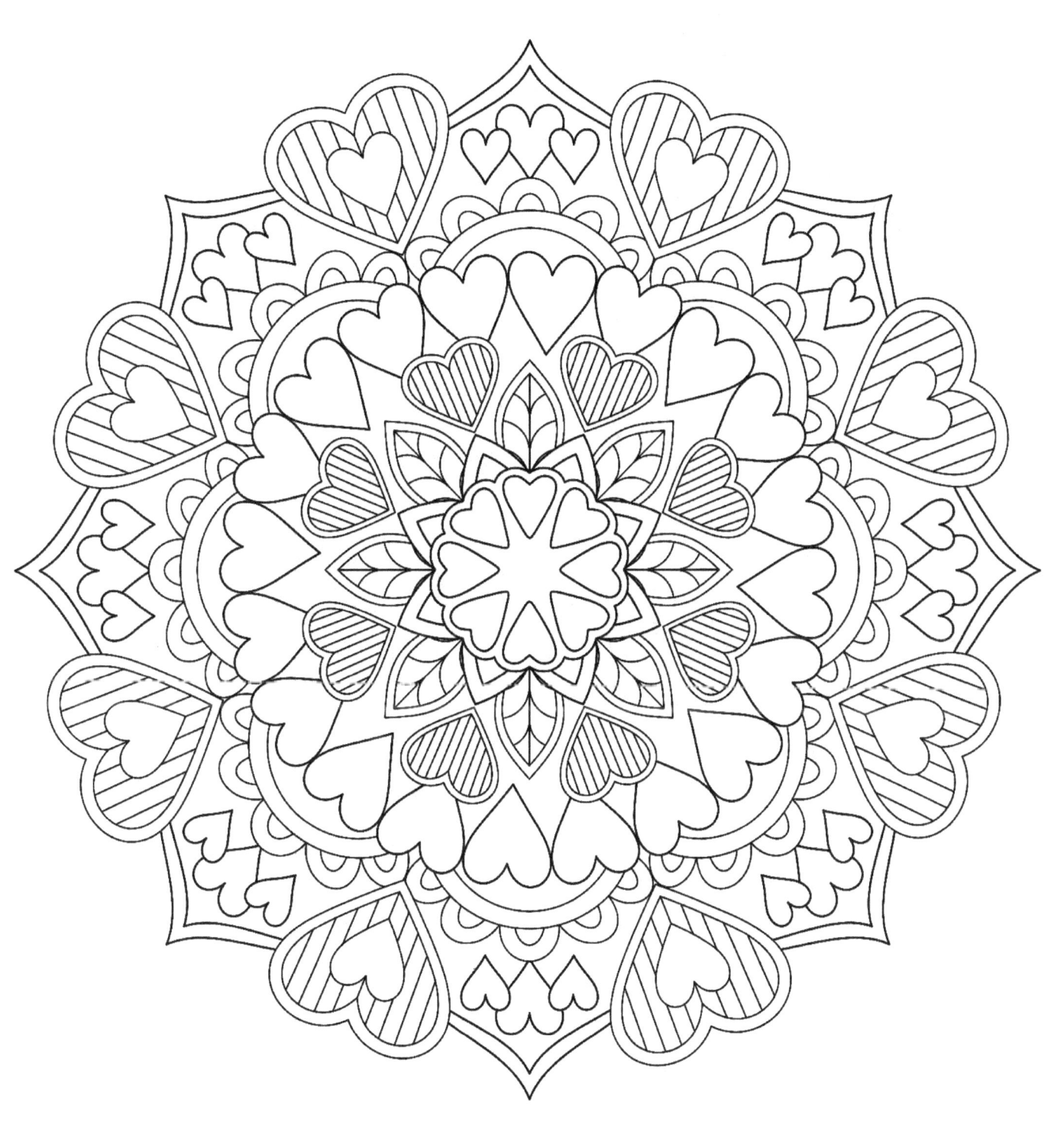

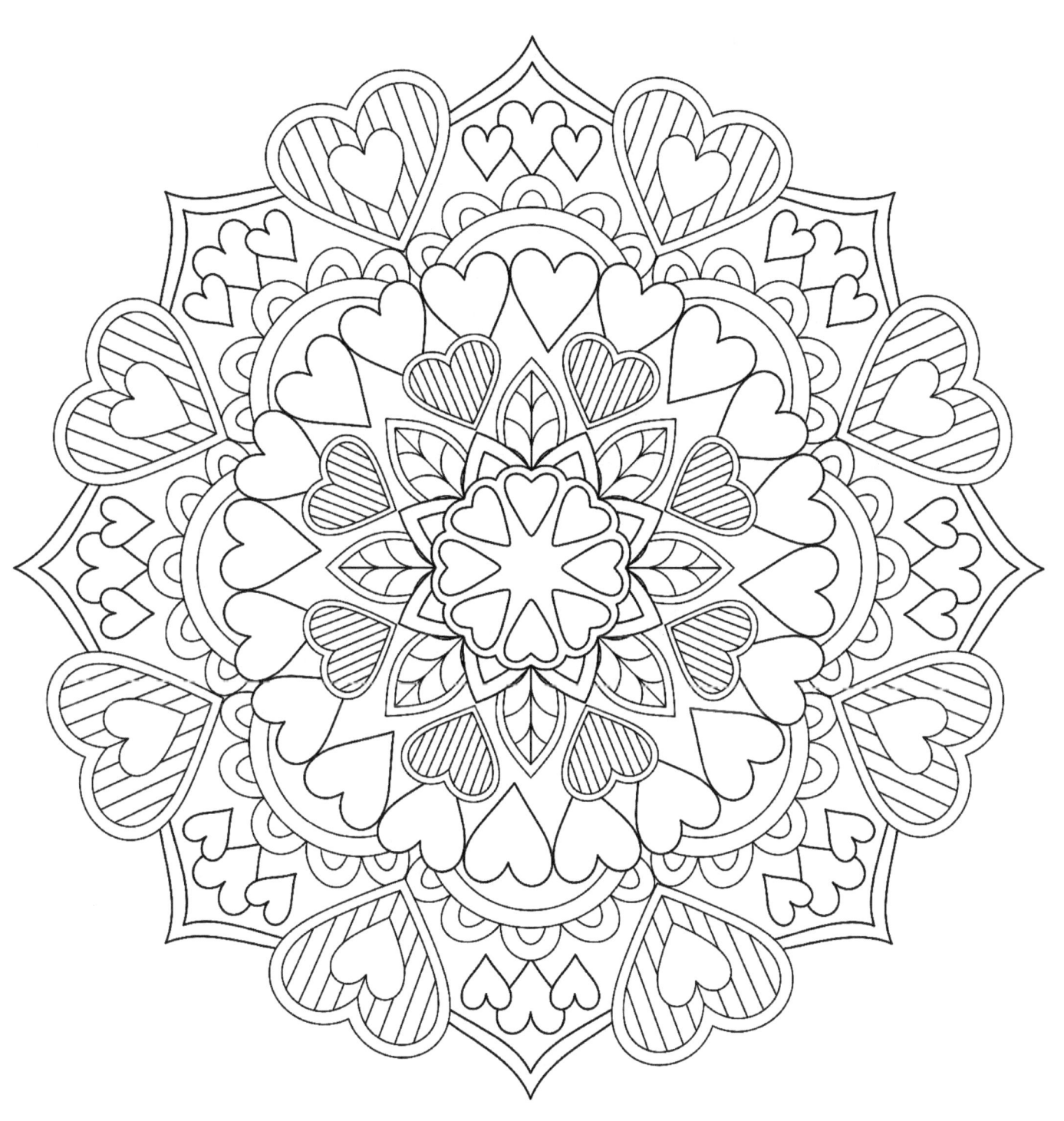

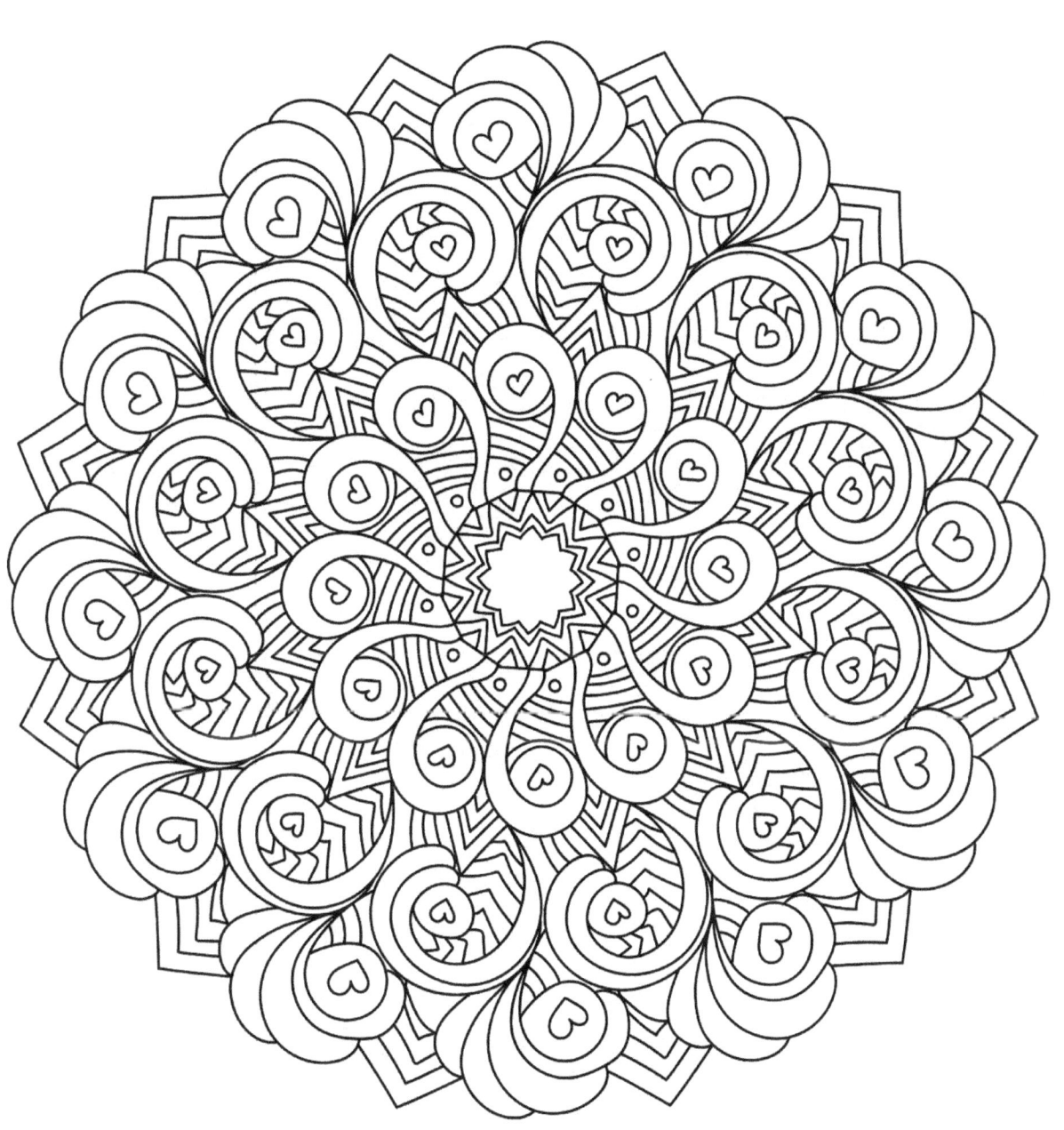

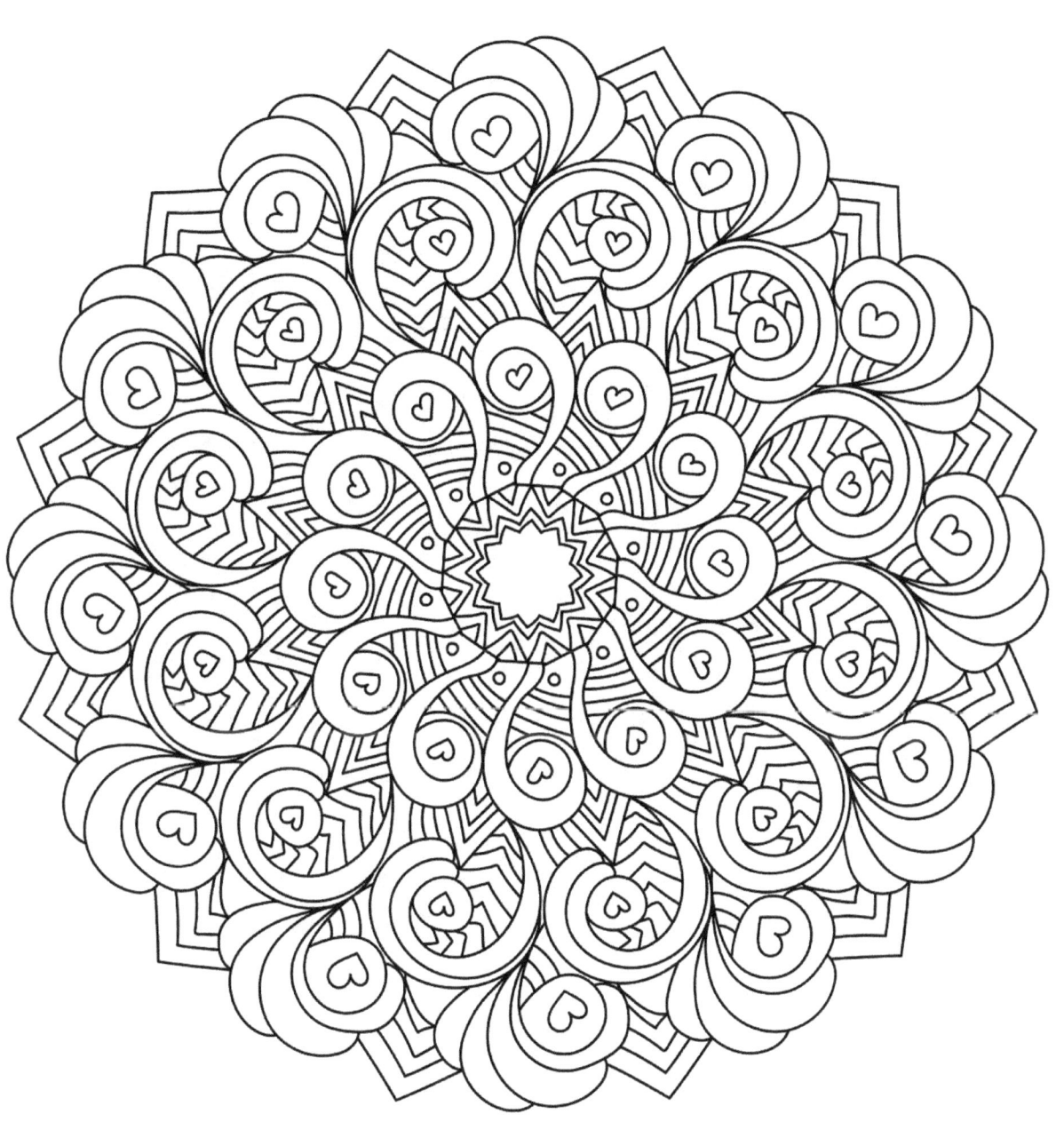

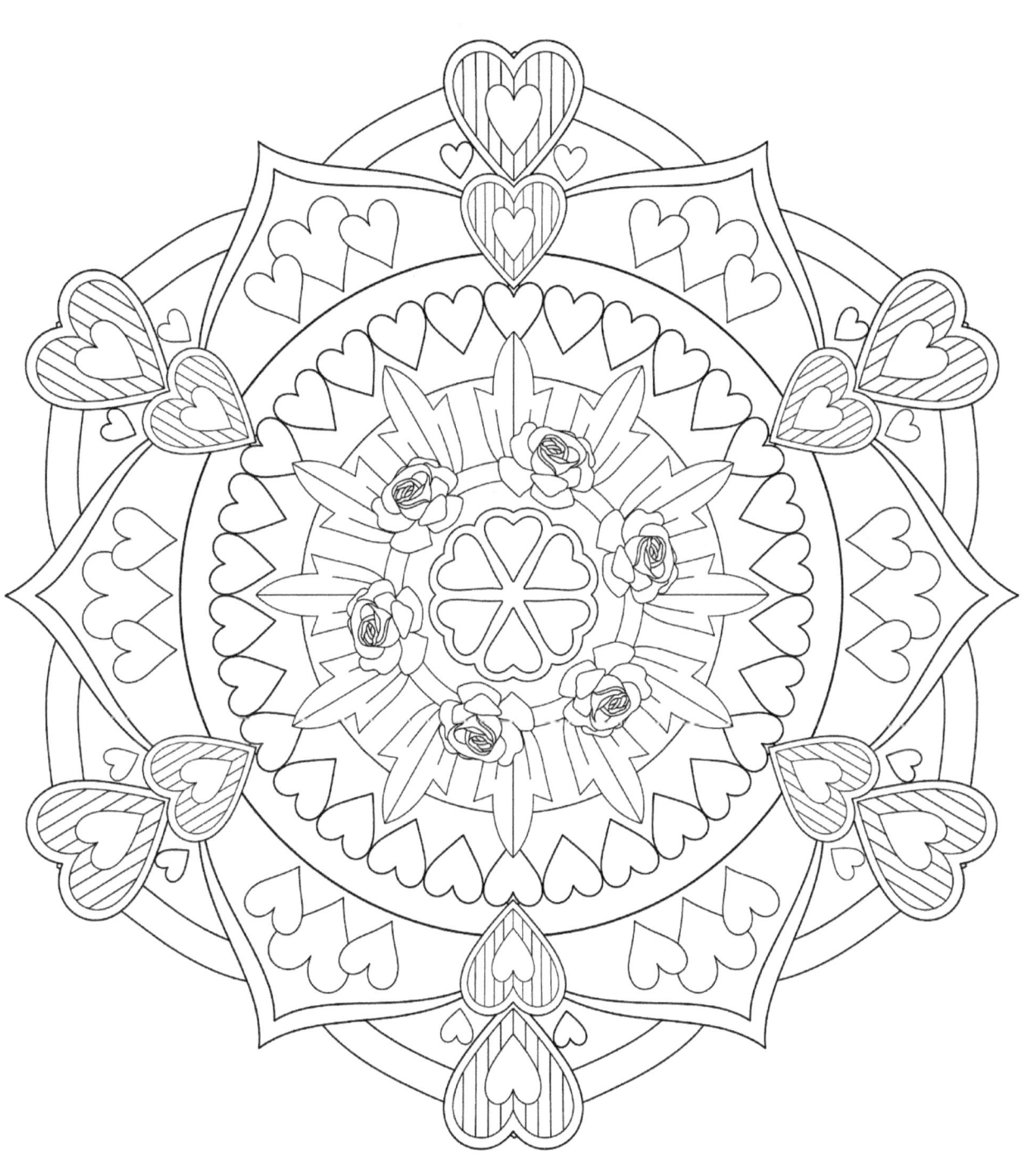

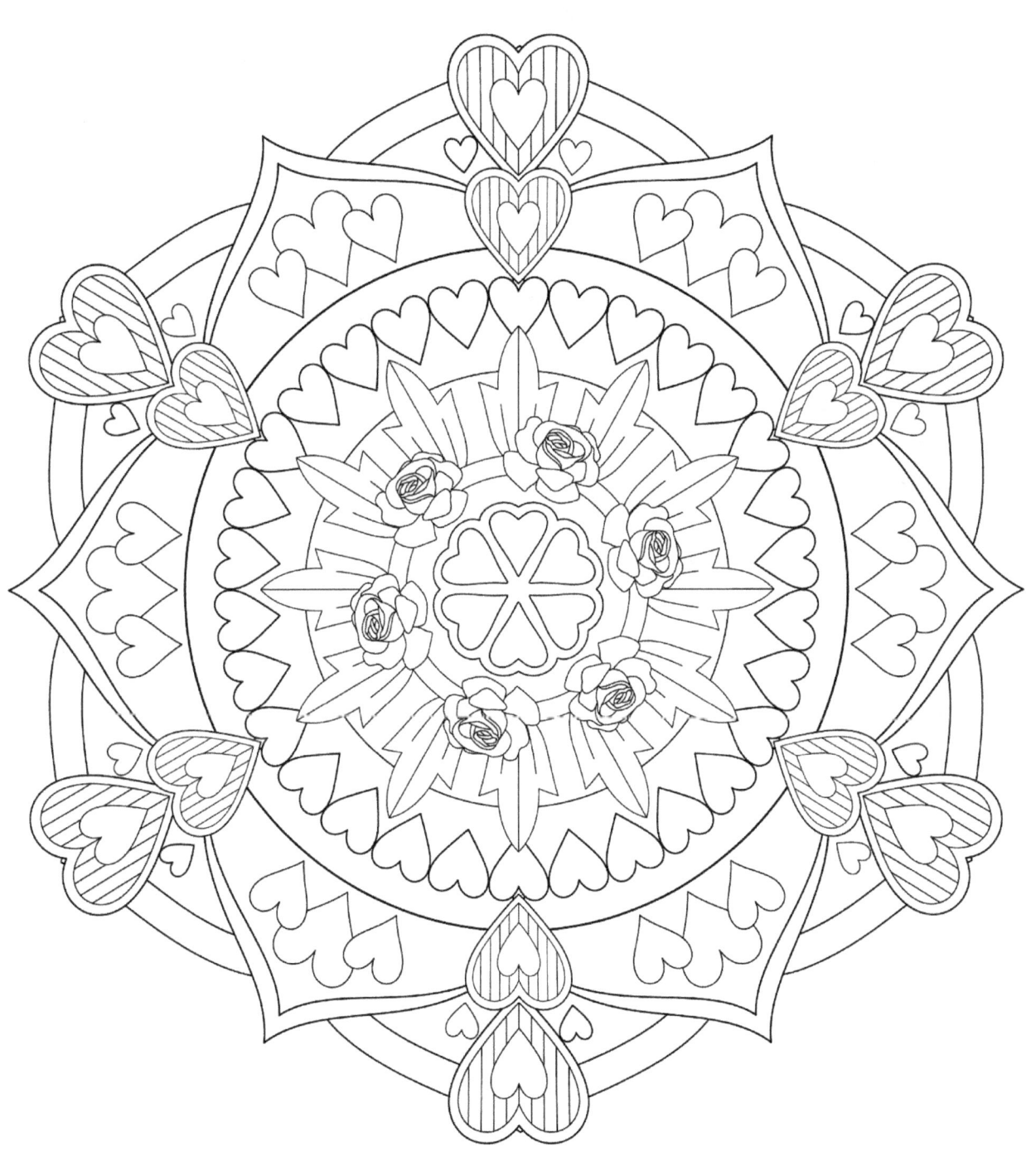

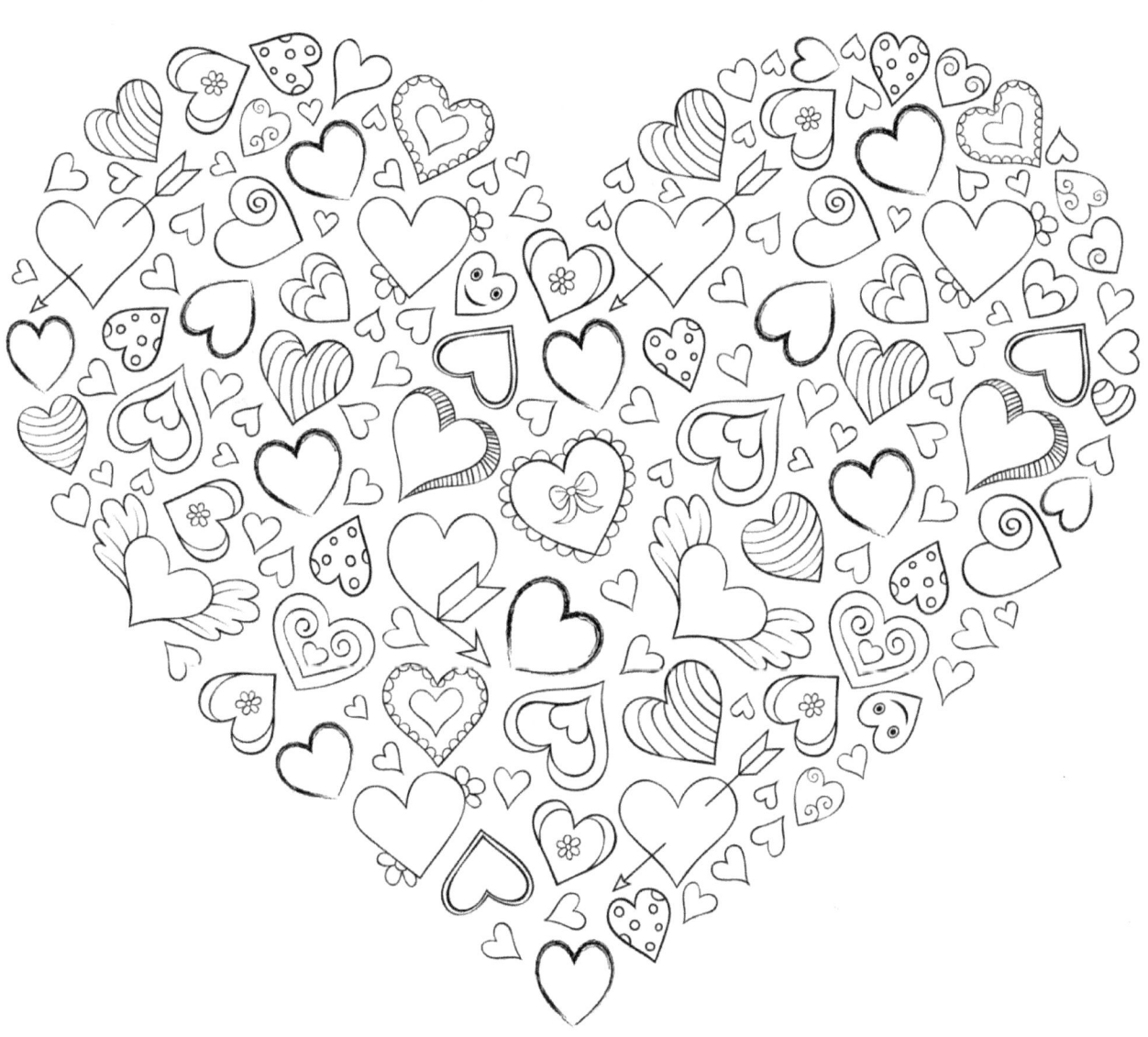

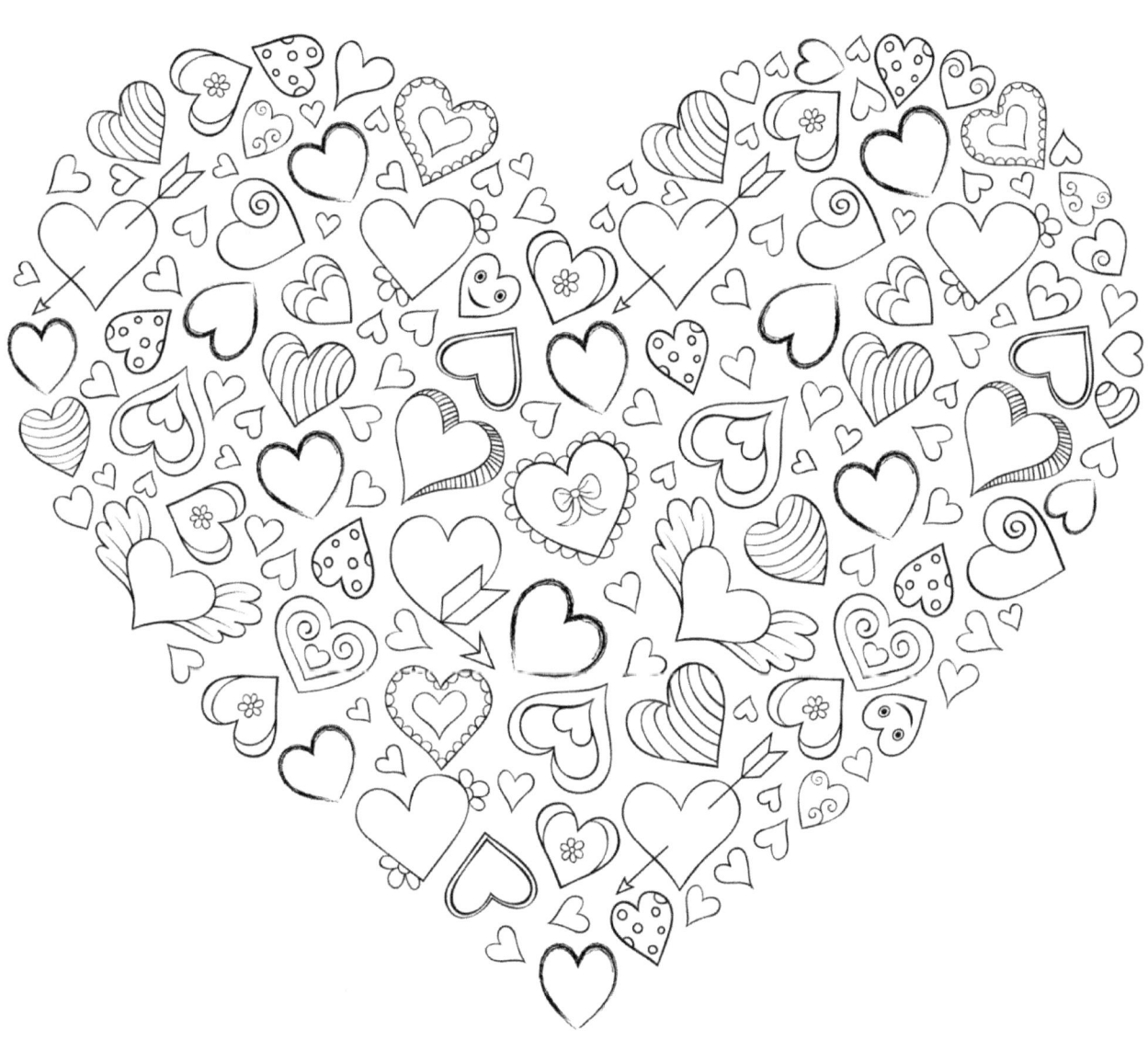

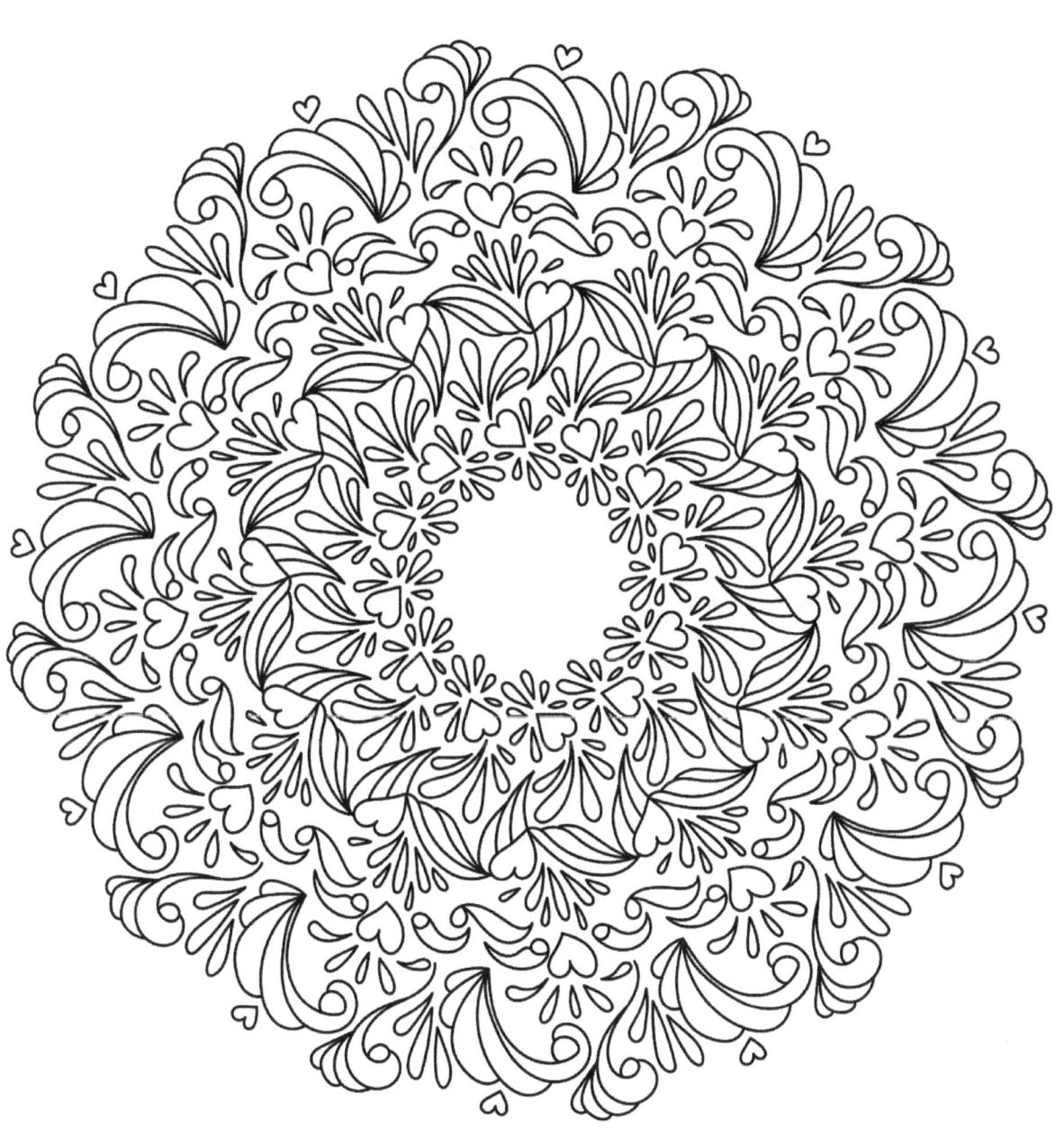

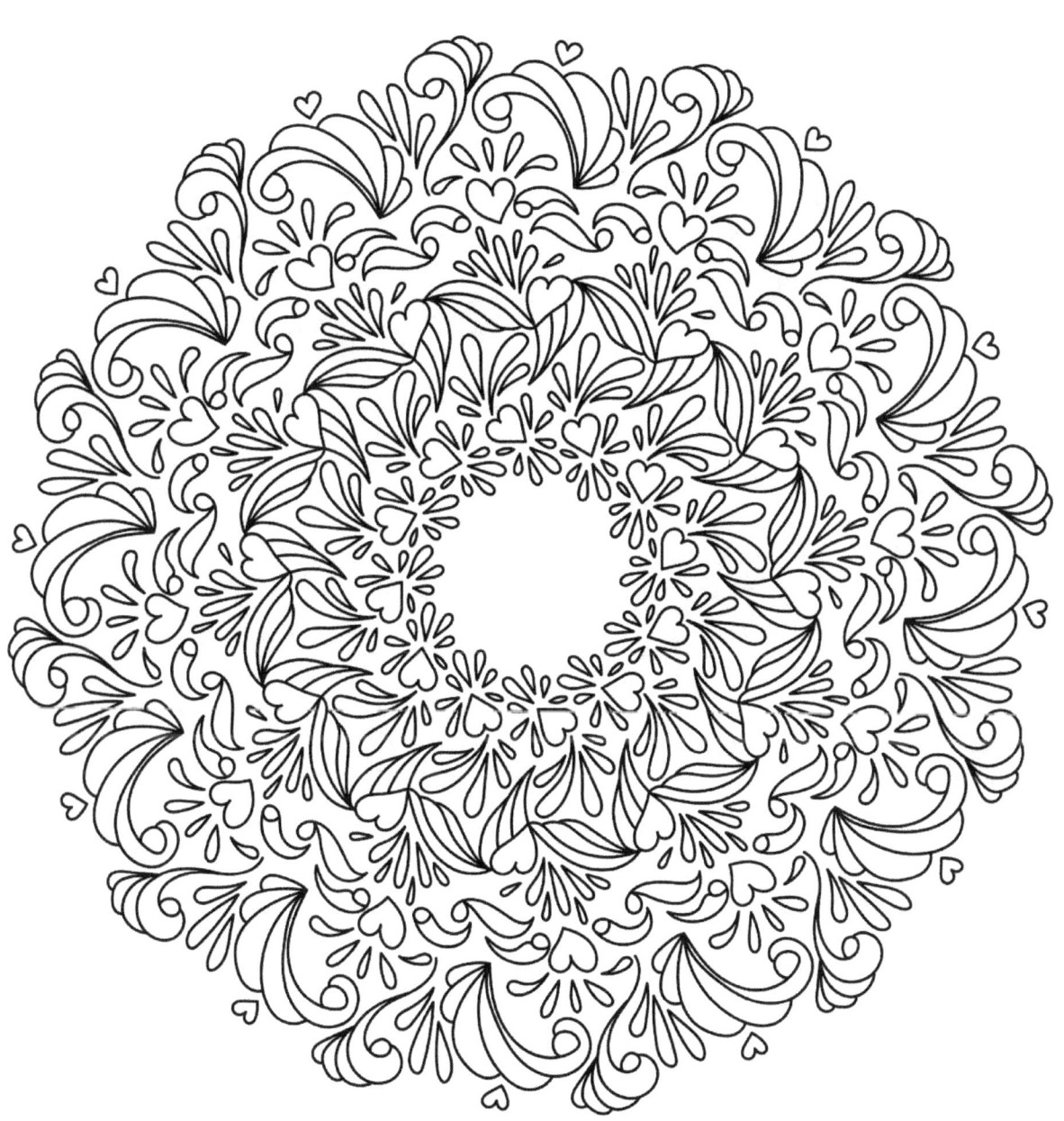

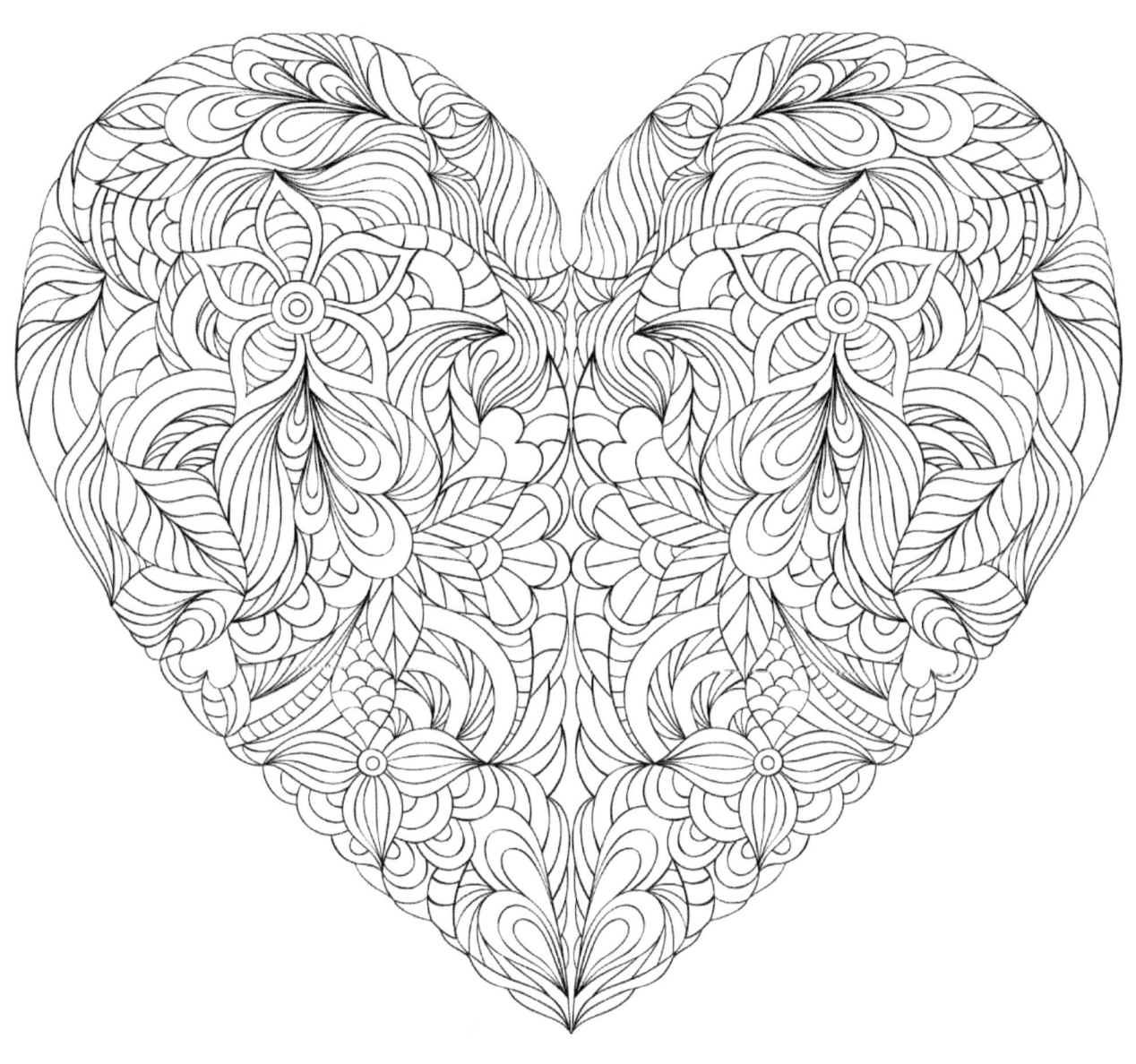

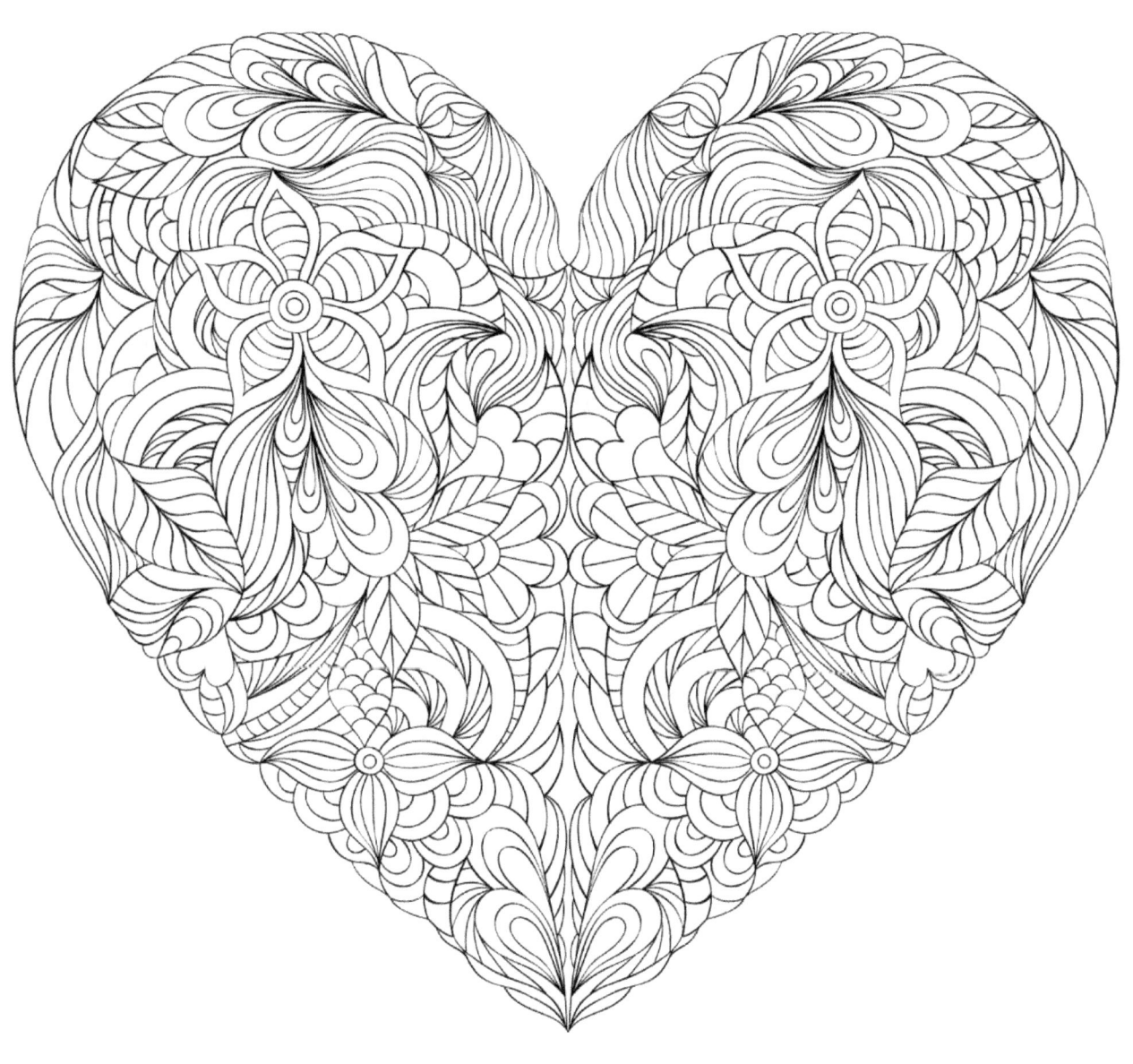

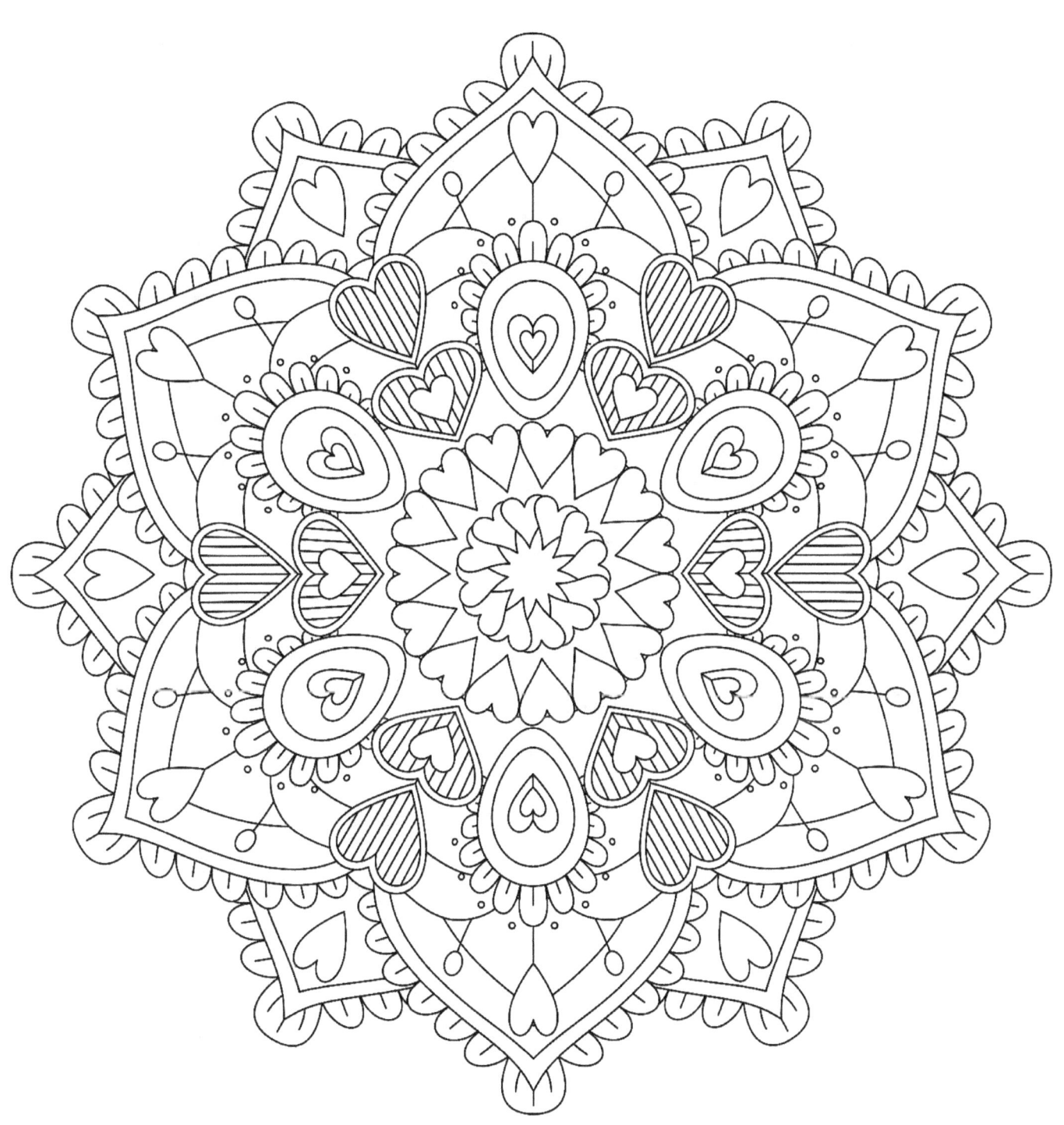

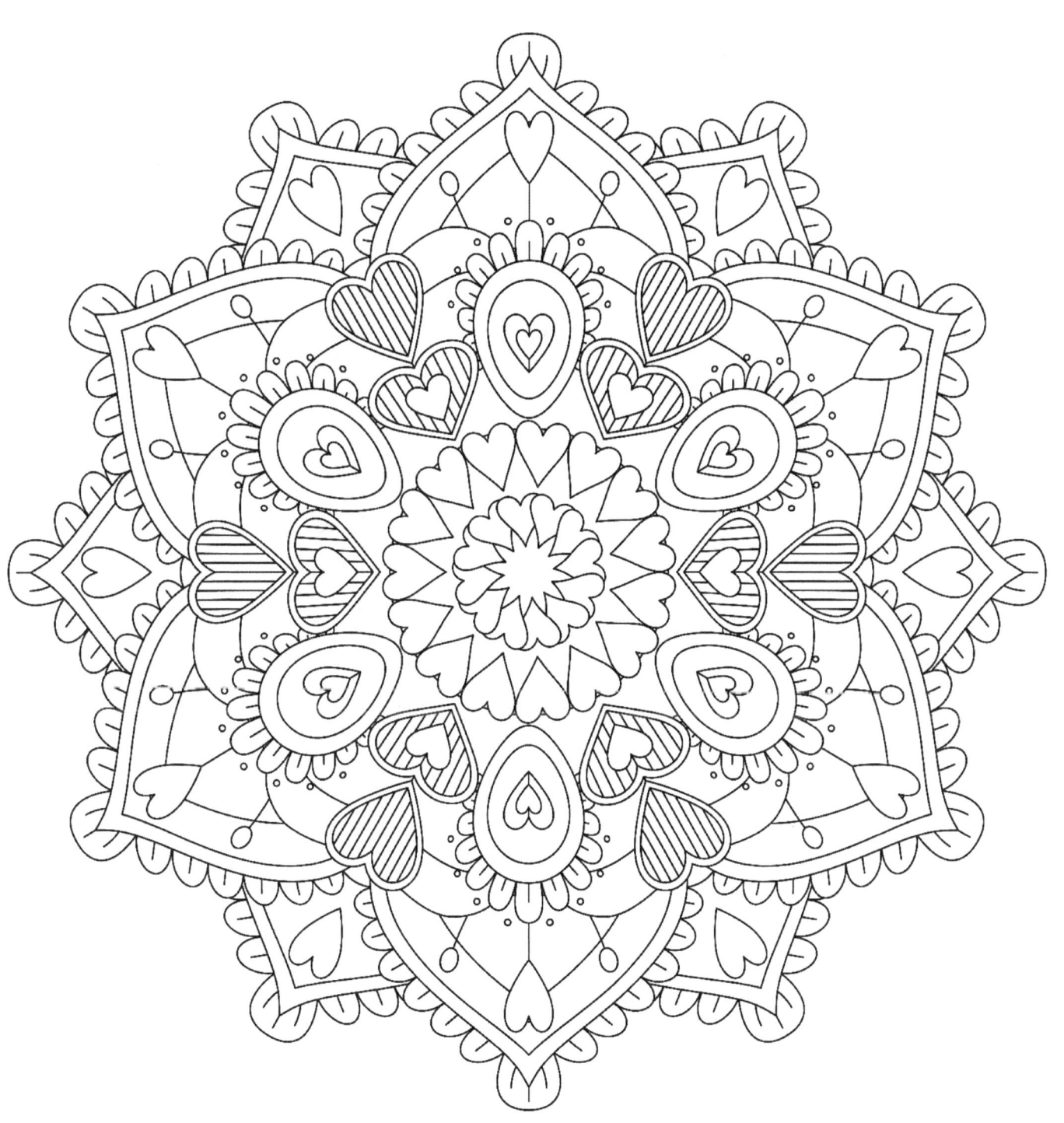

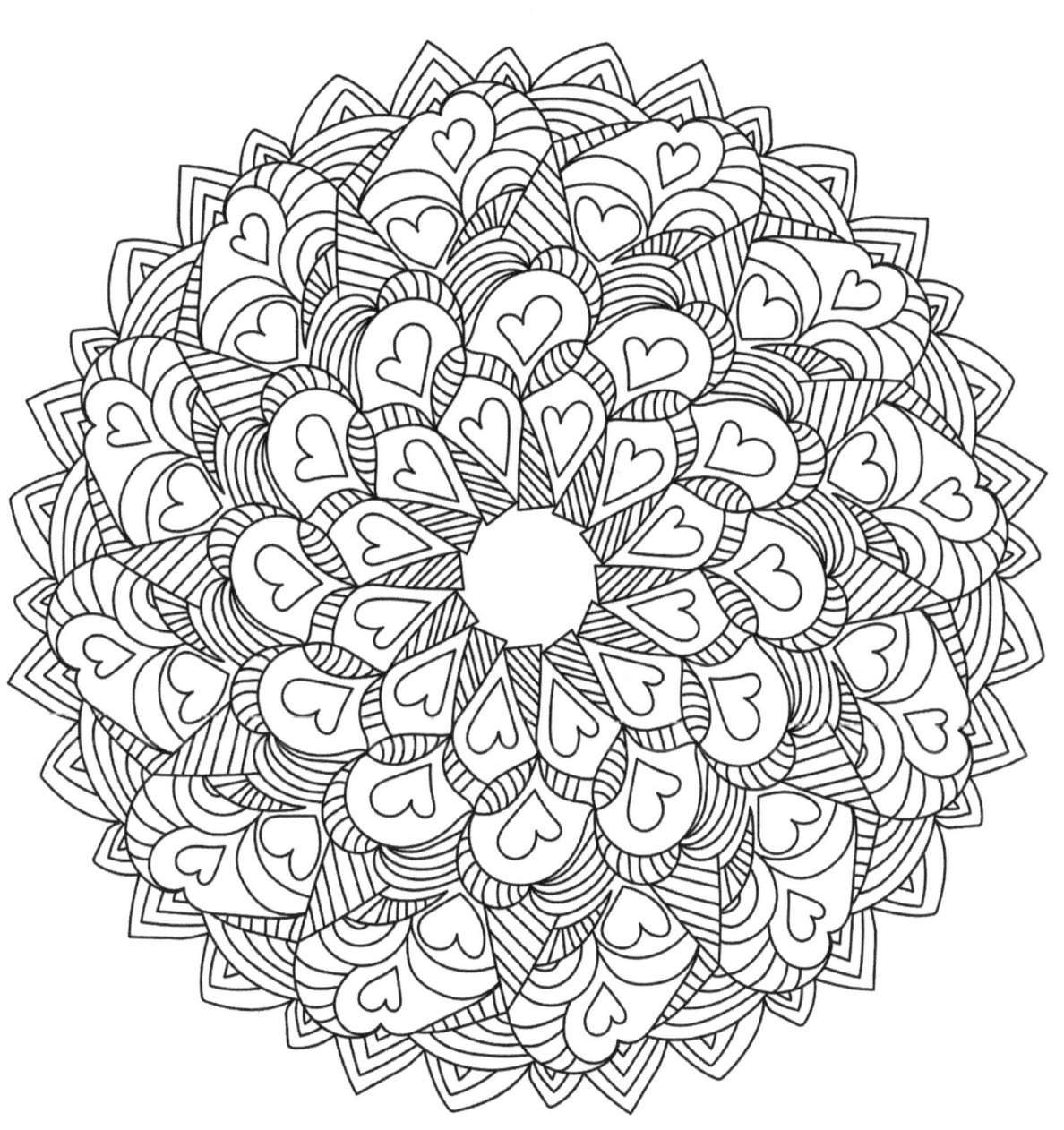

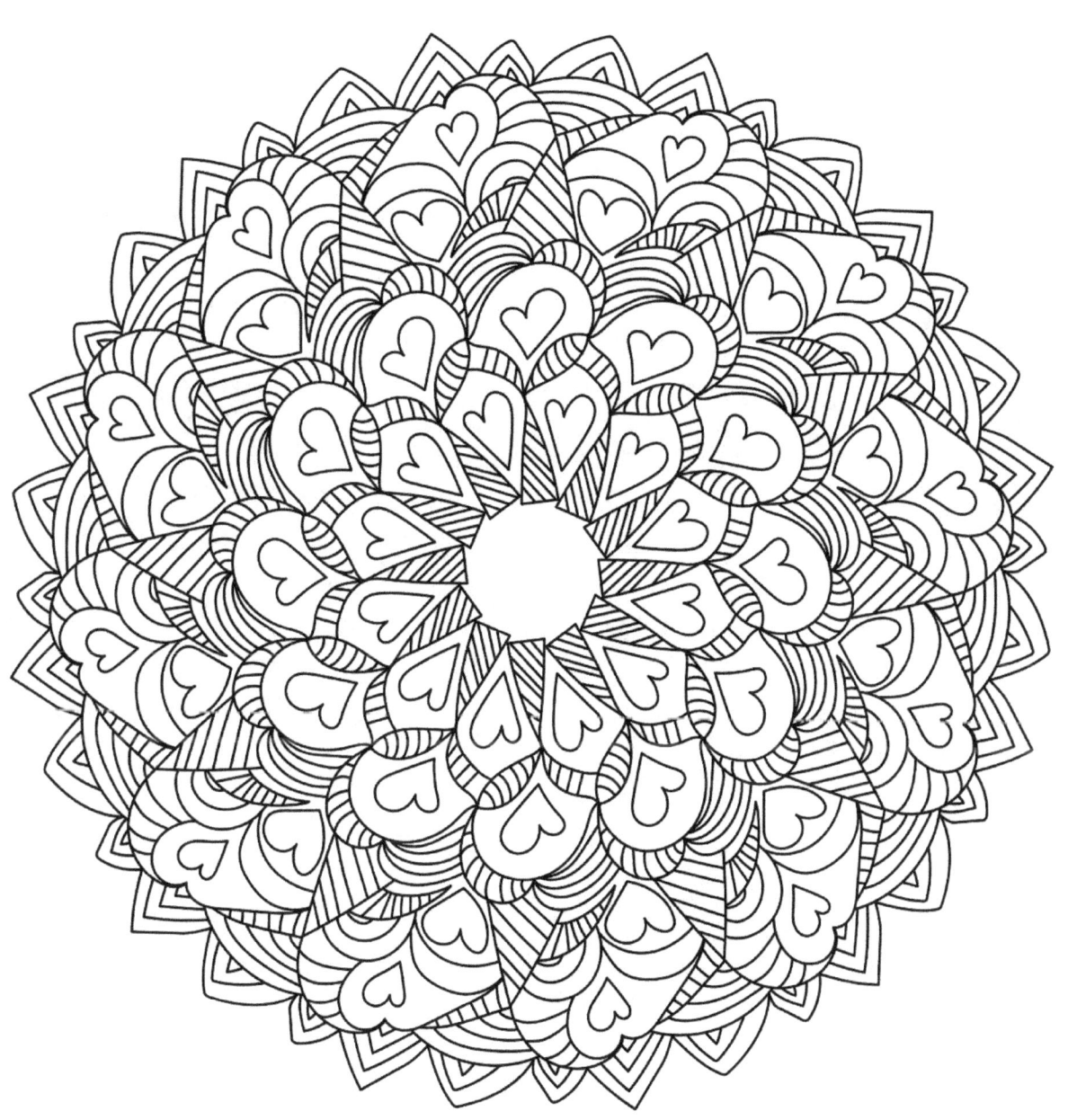

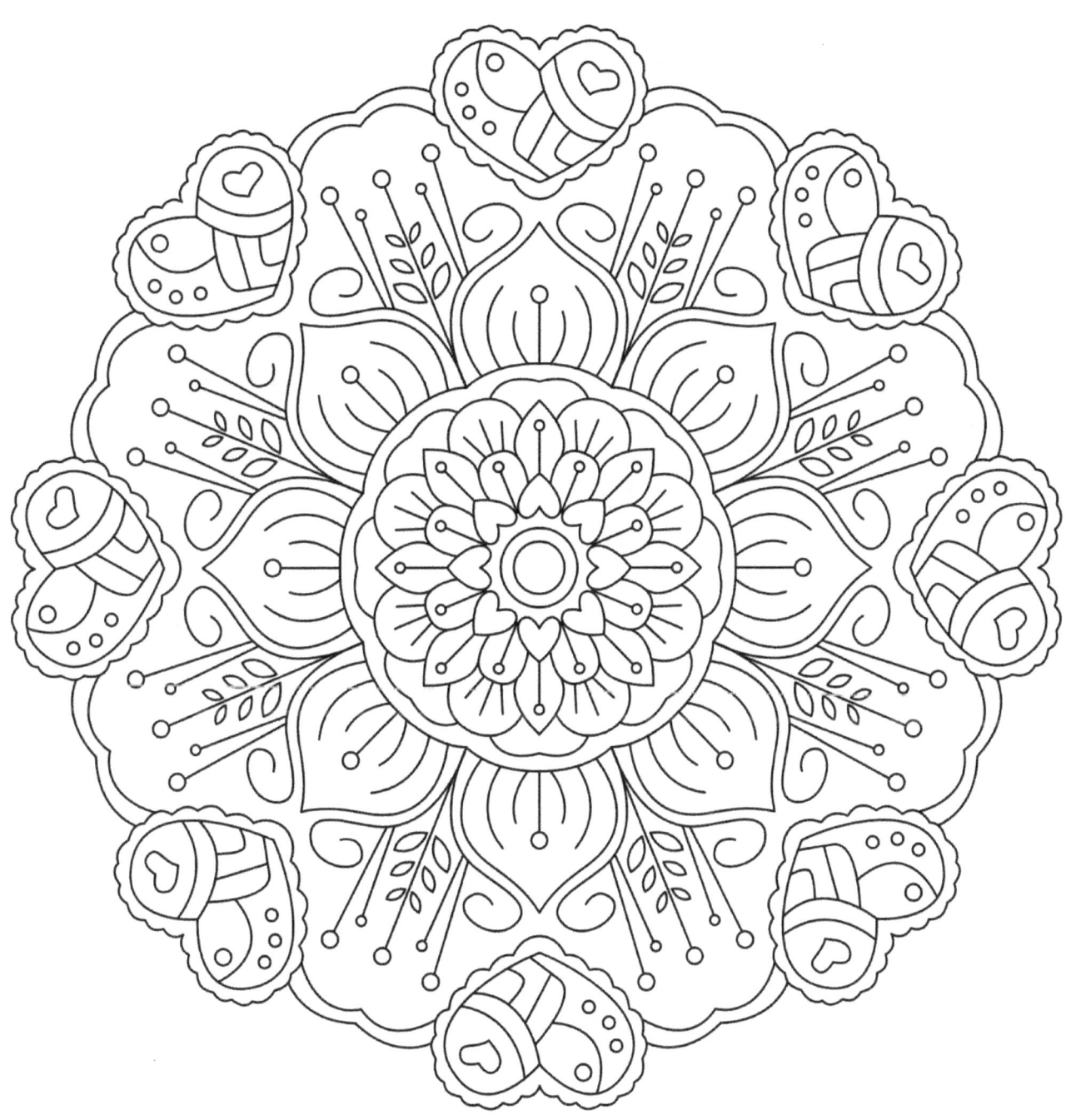

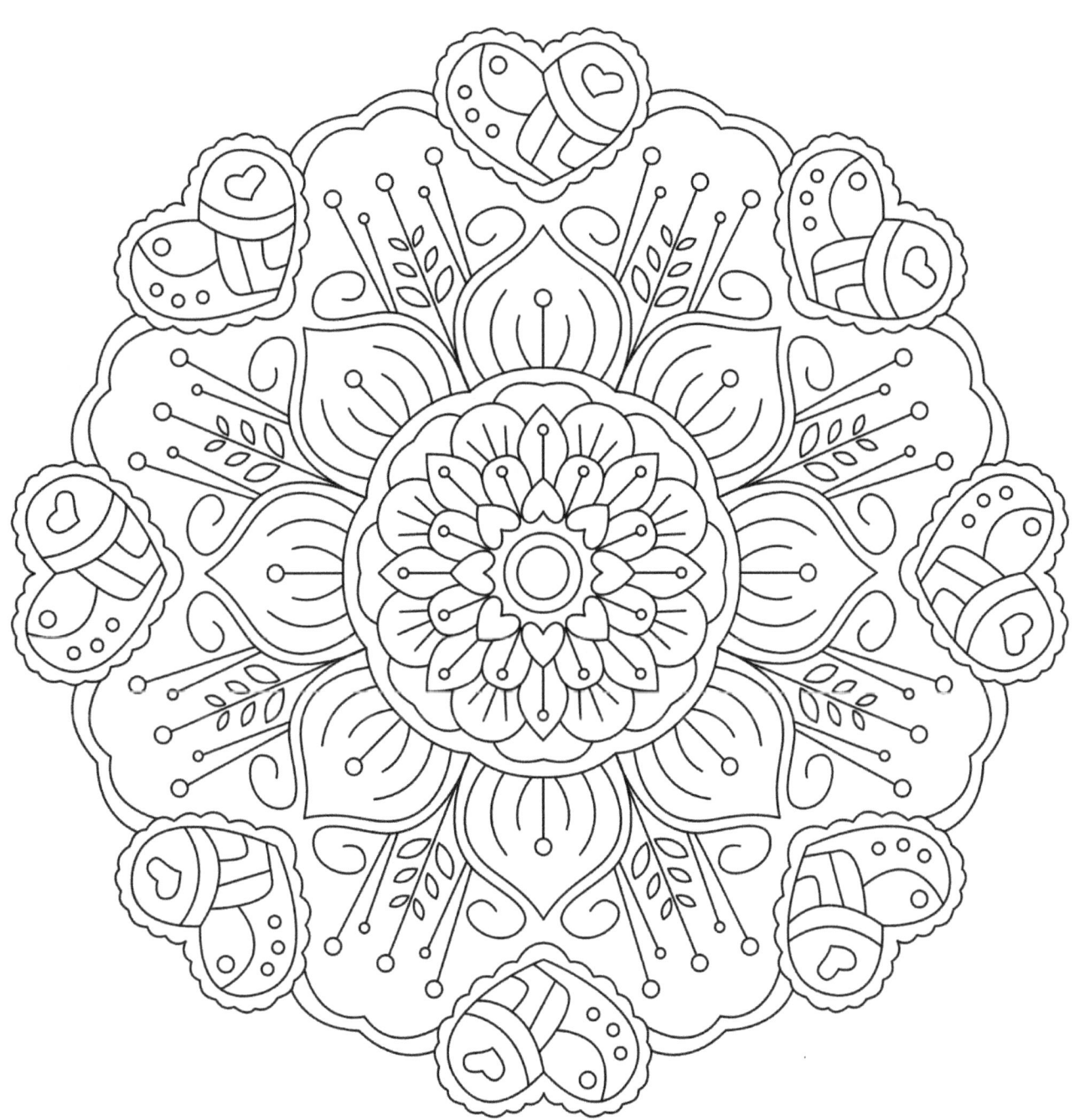